THEIRS IS
THE KINGDOM

THEIRS IS THE KINGDOM

The Wealth of the Windsors

ANDREW MORTON

MICHAEL O'MARA BOOKS LIMITED

TO ALEXANDRA AND LYDIA

£/$ conversion rates		
pre 1900	£ ≃	$5.00
1900	£ =	$4.84
1910	£ =	$4.84
1920	£ =	$4.42
1930	£ =	$4.86
1940	£ =	$3.83
1950	£ =	$2.80
1960	£ =	$2.80
1970	£ =	$2.40
1980	£ =	$2.32
Today	£ =	$1.70

First published in Great Britain by
Michael O'Mara Books Ltd
20 Queen Anne Street
London W1N 9FB

A CIP catalogue record for this book is available
from the British Library

ISBN 0-948397-23-3

Picture Research: Marion Pullen

FRONTISPIECE: *The Princess of Wales during her
visit to Saudi Arabia in 1986. Her diamond and
pearl tiara was a wedding gift from the Queen.*

Typeset by Florencetype Ltd, Kewstoke, Avon
Printed and bound in Spain by Cayfosa Industria
Grafica

Contents

1
Behold the Kingdom

The noise of the traffic crawling round Hyde Park corner fades to a dull murmur as you enter the tranquility of the Queen's private gardens at Buckingham Palace. Once inside the stone portals the sounds of the late twentieth century are replaced by the discreet rustle of a time when the horse-drawn carriage ruled the roads. Your guide, the Yeoman of the Silver Plate, produces a key from his waistcoat and opens a mahogany-fronted door that diplomatically disguises the solid steel hidden beneath. As the door shuts behind you, the world outside is left in abeyance. Now you are inside the New Area, halfway down to the basement. It is a large, workmanlike room dominated by two long wooden polishing tables. This is where the silver plate is burnished before a State banquet and where the men from Garrard, the Crown Jewellers, bring the Crown Jewels to be cleaned. Over the years a king's ransom of wealth has passed through here – but this is not your final destination.

In the corner is a solid metal grille. Once more a key is produced and the well-greased grille slides back to reveal an unprepossessing industrial lift. Yet another key opens the lift door. Nothing is left to chance for you are about to enter the last secret royal kingdom, a hidden realm of riches almost beyond comprehension. A land where the few visitors are awestruck by its splendour yet are immediately bound by a vow of silence.

OPPOSITE: *The splendid Colonnade clock egg acquired by Queen Mary after the fall of the Russian Romanov dynasty.* BELOW: *The gardens at Buckingham Palace, possibly the most valuable piece of undeveloped real estate in the world.*

The lift down takes an eternity, as the hiss from the hydraulics breaks the nervous silence. You feel as if you have sunk down hundreds of feet, but you are really no more than forty feet below ground level as you enter another world. Security is remorseless. You are ordered to remain by the lift while the Yeoman walks along a U-shaped corridor to the last hurdle, a fourteen-inch thick steel door protected by an intricate combination lock. A brick wall prevents the visitor from watching or hearing the dull clicks as the lock yields its secrets.

Finally the heavy portcullis swings back and the strip lights are switched on. Behold the royal kingdom. You have penetrated the heart of the mystery surrounding the House of Windsor and its fabulous fortune. However, this is the very antithesis of a mythical Aladdin's Cave where diamonds twinkle in the half light and blood red rubies and creamy pearls spill from their chests. No, the hidden royal fortune has all the romance of a balance sheet as it lies in glorious chaos beneath thick plastic sheets on rank upon rank of cheap white shelving. Yet the very disorder is a silent tribute to a family who maintain such a blithe insouciance to their awesome inheritance. 'There is nothing here as common as gold bars,' says one senior member of staff. 'It has been in the family for generations. This is their secret storeroom.'

This royal wealth of ages is stored in a disused air raid shelter in a series of white-walled rooms covering an area the size of an ice rink. Jewelled scabbards from the East lie alongside the Great Seals of Office, which in turn give way to diamond-encrusted snuff boxes and a veritable zoo of exquisitely carved Fabergé animals. These were but amusing trinkets collected by the beautiful Queen Alexandra in the days when Russia still had a Tsar. Under the sheeting sits an obsidian sacred baboon, its rose diamond eyes glinting, and a gun-metal Indian elephant with cabochon ruby eyes and ivory tusks, a Christmas day gift to King George V from his family. While the craftsmanship of Carl Fabergé delights the eye in spite of the incongruous setting (much of the royal collection is at Sandringham), it is the sheer scale of the precious royal heritage which is so impressive. As one member of the Royal Household recalls, 'You simply cannot take it all in. It is mind numbing.'

RIGHT: *The west front of Buckingham Palace.*

*The plate and silverware given to Princess
Elizabeth and Prince Philip as wedding presents.*

Huge Georgian soup tureens which require
two men to lift them, great silver shields and
platters, the silver candelabra which the Duke
of Edinburgh gave to the Queen to celebrate
their silver wedding anniversary, gold snuff
boxes, ornamental cutlasses encrusted with
precious stones, ivory figures chased with silver
and gold, the weighty St George and the Dragon
silver table display which is ceremoniously
exhibited for State banquets, and memorabilia
from the days of Napoleon and Nelson. Three

huge red moroccan leather volumes, stamped
with Queen Victoria's initials, catalogue this
cornucopia of riches. Every item was labelled
and photographed from every angle so that no
one was in any doubt as to its ownership.
Queen Victoria left nothing to chance. She
guarded her heritage jealously.

Nonetheless, jewelled rings and necklaces
together with uncut emerals lie scattered hap-
hazardly on shelves. Are these the legendary
Indian emeralds, given by Maharajahs and
Nizams in tribute to the British royal family at
the height of their Imperial spendour? These
jewels, which have exerted a fascination for

historians, have been well hidden down the years. Their existence first came to light when a number of uncut emeralds were left in the Duchess of Windsor's jewellery box which was found abandoned on Sunningdale golf course during a daring daylight robbery in 1946.

This disused air raid shelter, which the Queen occasionally inspects, harbours but a proportion of the royal riches and yet the discovery of this uncharted room gives an indication of the sheer scale of the wealth of the House of Windsor. Like an iceberg, so much of the royal fortune is submerged beneath the eyes of the world. It is surrounded by dispute as to how much of this vast fortune is owned by the Queen and her family and how much is held in trust for the nation.

The confusion has merely added to the fable surrounding the Queen who is often described as the 'world's richest woman'. Over the years estimates of her private fortune have varied from a hardly believable £2 million ($4.8 million) in 1971 advanced by the monarch's loyal servant, Sir Richard Colville, to under £50 million ($120 million) by her former Lord Chamberlain, the late Lord Cobbold in the same year, or £2.4 billion ($4.08 billion), £3.34 billion ($5.67 billion) and £15.3 billion ($26.01 billion), depending on which financial magazine you subscribe to. In 1985 the excitable Sunday tabloid, the *News of the World*, trumpeted that the Queen's fortune increased by £700,000 ($1,190,000) a day or £486.11p ($826) a minute.

Perhaps we may use the 'clock index' as a whimsical guide to illustrate the awesome dimensions of the royal possessions. The German industrialist, Prince Thurn und Taxis, ranked twenty-second in the world's hierarchy of the super rich, employs one man at his glorious palace of Schloss St Emmeram at Regensburg in Bavaria whose sole role in life is to wind up the clocks. At Buckingham Palace the Queen has two men on her staff to do that job. There is even a glossy book, priced £60 ($102), devoted to Her Majesty's clock collection – 'my sweet musicians' as Queen Elizabeth the Queen Mother, describes her own elegant pieces.

Princess Elizabeth's presents included a diamond festoon scroll tiara from Queen Mary.

ABOVE: *The Queen's Silver Jubilee gifts included loyal addresses and a carved elephant's tusk.*

We live in a world of price tags where everything from the electricity industry to the National Health Service is regarded as a saleable commodity. Can it be long before the monarchy, which for so long has lain like an Old Master gathering dust in the family attic, is assessed, stripped and sold off? Certainly the Crown Estates, valued at £1.2 billion ($2.04 billion), are prime candidates for the current pressure to privatize. One of the tasks of this book is to assess just how much the Queen and the rest of the royal family are really worth, by attempting to tease out the threads of national holdings like the Crown Jewels and Royal Collections, and distinguishing these from the royal family's private possessions. By tracing these elements back through the years the Windsor heritage can be seen in all its dynastic glory.

The astonishing rise of the House of Windsor since Queen Victoria's accession in 1837 is all the more remarkable when it is recalled that at

OPPOSITE: *Arab sheiks such as the Emir of Bahrain continue to lavish tribute on the Windsors.*

her coronation all Queen Victoria possessed was a legacy of debt inherited from her impecunious predecessors. In just 150 years the Windsors, from being £50,000 ($250,000) in debt, are now billionaires. The Queen's holdings in land, jewellery, fine art collections, including the Fabergé holdings, thoroughbreds, cars, together with a portfolio of stocks and shares give a private fortune of between £1 ($1.72) and £1.2 billion ($2.04 billion) at 1989 prices, while the Prince of Wales is among the richest people in Britain with a fortune of over £275 million ($467.5 million).

The royal family's growth to become perhaps the most influential financial dynasty in the world has been accomplished by a measure of astute judgement and advice, sound investment and great good fortune, together with the most precious gift that can be bestowed, the absence of taxation.

It has been no ordinary royal progress where, as with the oil-rich Sultan of Brunei and the Middle Eastern potentates, wealth can be traced to a solitary source. The bequest of £250,000 ($1,250,000) to Queen Victoria from a miserly eccentric and the astonishing luck of Queen Mary's grandfather, the Duke of Cambridge, who in 1808 won a casket of emeralds in a

ABOVE: *The wedding glassware given to Princess Elizabeth included engraved plates from America.*

Frankfurt lottery, are but two examples of the haphazard way the wealth of the Windsor dynasty has been accumulated.

Land holdings and lucrative marriages have been the traditional methods for the European aristocracy to maintain their wealth and privileges. Many of their estates, like those of the Duke of Westminster, have survived the depredations of systematic taxation and social revolution. Curiously, the rise of the Windsors since Queen Victoria has not depended on land alone. While the Duchies of Lancaster and Cornwall have provided a substantial income over the years, they have not been the mainstay of the royal fortune. Today the Queen's estates at Balmoral and Sandringham are but a small part of her overall wealth.

Nor have the Windsors sustained their evolution by ambitious marriages. Quite the opposite. One of the features of the Windsor dynasty has been the impoverished position of those who married into the family. In an age when many British aristocratic families like the Roxburghes and Marlboroughs maintained their line by marriage into wealthy American families, the Windsors, whether by accident or design, have never subscribed to this process.

In her youth the family of Princess May of Teck, later Queen Mary, was forced to flee the country because of debts, while Princess Alexandra, after her marriage to the Prince of Wales, had a dress allowance which was twelve times greater than her father's annual income at the Danish court.

When Prince Philip married Princess Elizabeth he had two suits to his name and left for his wedding at Westminster Abbey wearing darned socks. During one of his early visits to Balmoral he had to borrow a kilt from the royal stock. It was so short that he dropped a curtsey

OPPOSITE: *An impoverished Prince Philip brought little wealth into the Windsors but much energy.*

Prince Charles in his powerful speedboat given to him by Imelda Marcos, wife of the deposed Philippines President. He later donated it to a youth organization.

to King George VI who was distinctly un-impressed by this breach of protocol.

The commoners who have played and con-tinue to play such a remarkable part in the fortunes of the Windsors – notably Lady Elizabeth Bowes-Lyon, Lady Diana Spencer, Wallis Simpson, Antony Armstrong-Jones and Sarah Ferguson – have brought little but their personalities into the royal family.

However, the youthful deprivations of Queen Victoria, Queen Mary and Prince Philip have perhaps provided the drive combined with caution necessary to consolidate the dynasty. The royal 'disease' of conspicuous consumption finds its only example in the Windsor family with the switchback fortunes of King Edward VII. The other notable exception to the Windsor tradition of frugality was Edward VIII. The Abdication and his personal excesses – even in 1960 he was spending £7,500 ($21,000) a month on clothes for the 63-year-old Duchess – severely dislocated the family's orderly financial progress.

While savings from the Privy Purse and the Civil List – the annual contribution made from Parliament to the royal family – have played their part, particularly during Queen Victoria's reign, the Windsors have bolstered their rise by the acceptance of tribute on a level rarely seen since the days of the Spanish Empire and the plunder of South American silver mines.

By an accident of history they have ruled during a period when Great Britain's star was ascendant on the world stage, accepting gifts from every corner of the globe, particularly the Indian subcontinent. Yet while they were showered with pearls, sapphires and diamonds on a majestic scale, not every offering has added to the splendour of their heritage. When Edward VII moved into Buckingham Palace following his accession, he was horrified to discover a room filled with yellowing elephant tusks. During the present reign, the Queen has been given everything from a 1300-lb elephant to a crocodile in a biscuit tin.

Paradoxically, the Victorian period onwards has seen a waning of royal power, a factor which has merely added to the Windsors'

OPPOSITE: *The Princess of Wales wears her wedding gift of a suite of diamond and sapphires.*

While envy and avarice are the traditional handmaidens of great wealth, the predominant feature with the Windsors has been a sustained secrecy associated with their remarkable fortune. Yet this has occurred during a period of unprecedented expansion in the public pomp and circumstance surrounding the monarchy. It is notable, for example, that before 1837 royal wills were public documents, available for inspection by all and sundry. In this seemingly democratic age, every royal will from Victoria onwards has been sealed from the eyes of the world. They are held in a gun-metal safe behind an iron cage on the first floor of Somerset House. Even long-serving civil servants are discouraged from visiting this secret place. This is truly the heart of the darkness surrounding the royal family and their great wealth.

As they have become a more private family, their continuing constitutional position has enabled them to sustain their financial privileges — entitlements founded on their civic role. Their public power may have waned, but their private influence has remained considerable and has underpinned the development of the Windsor fortune. Over the last 150 years Parliament has constructed a sturdy fence of legislation around the Windsors protecting their wills, stocks and shares and estates from the eyes of the world. Most recently, the Queen has been exempted from the payment of the controversial community charge, a privilege which means that for the first time in recent royal history she is now free of any form of taxation. Until now the Queen has been obliged to pay rates on her estates of Balmoral and Sandringham. However, other members of the royal family will pay the charge.

Ironically, while the traditional power of the monarch has diminished, the international status of the British royal family has never been higher. The Windsors seem to stand taller because so many European royal families have vanished from the world stage. In the nineteeth century the British royal family competed with their European counterparts, particularly the German Kaiser, while in the late twentieth century they are in the ascendant. As ex-King Farouk of Egypt once observed, 'By the end of the century there will be only five royal Houses

ABOVE: *The Tsar and Tsarina wearing traditional Imperial Court costume of the Middle Ages. Note the Tsar's striking resemblance to King George V.*

personal wealth. When the Sun King, Louis XIV, made his grandiloquent remark, *L'état, c'est moi* ('I am the state'), he was merely giving voice to the status of European royalty in the seventeenth century. The notion that the monarch had or was even entitled to a private persona did not start to find expression until the eighteenth century. It was during the reign of Queen Victoria that the line between family life and public service was more clearly defined, drawing a corresponding distinction between public and private domains which finds its fullest expression during this reign.

OPPOSITE: *On the eve of war in 1913 George V and Queen Mary attended the wedding of the Kaiser's daughter in Berlin.*

Thus the Windsors are the only remaining feudal family to receive financial homage from rich and poor alike. The psychology of giving to the world's richest woman exerts its own fascination. Hence the prosperous, especially the *nouveau riche*, give in order to be dusted with royal status and to demonstrate publicly their own wealth, while the impoverished perhaps still cling to the folk memory of the divinity of kings, that their generosity to the monarch will help pave the way to God.

Royal weddings are the most vivid example. Princess Elizabeth's wedding gifts were valued in 1947 at around £500,000 ($2 million) and included a 2,000-year-old necklace from ex-King Farouk and ninety-six rubies set in gold from the Burmese people. The Princess of Wales was similarly showered with millions of pounds worth of gifts, including a suite of sapphires from the Crown Prince of Saudi Arabia. Jewellery is the traditional wedding endowment from the monarch to his or her family. However, Queen Mary so loved her possessions that she found the custom painful to keep. Her great niece, Lady Mary Whitley, recalls how she visited the old Queen who had promised her a casket of jewels as a wedding present. She kept the young girl on tenterhooks as she gave a rambling homily about the virtues of work, never once referring to her considerable gift. Finally, almost as an afterthought, she dispatched a servant to bring the heirlooms and handed them over with murmurings of regret to the trembling bride.

The royal attitude towards this endless stream of tribute occasionally borders on the blasé. Princess Alice, Duchess of Gloucester, displayed an effortless nonchalance towards her gifts following her marriage to George V's third son, Prince Henry, Duke of Gloucester. She recalls:

An Egyptian necklace dating back more than 2,000 years given by King Farouk to Princess Elizabeth on her wedding day. She received an estimated £500,000 ($2.5 million) worth of presents.

I began to write letters to the 1,200 or so people and organizations who had been kind enough to give us presents. We had received so many lovely things: silver and splendid jewellery from the King and Queen, the various wedding cakes, a white ostrich-feather wrap from the Ostrich Farmers of South Africa and a Standard car which we felt we had to return to the donor. We were to receive lots of presents in the years to come, many of them rather useless things like elephant tusks, which we hid away till the donor called and then fished out again so as not to give offence.

left: clubs, diamonds, hearts, spades and Windsor.'

This often brutal harvest of royalty has had two main influences on the Windsors. Firstly they have benefitted from the break-up of European royal families by buying up their collections, notably Queen Mary's bargain basement purchase of the fabulous Imperial jewels smuggled out of Russia during the Revolution. Secondly, as the British Empire has faded away, the royal family has been sustained and celebrated as a unique international institution. Longevity has its rewards.

The most lavish presentations were probably those made by shipping companies when one launched one of their ships. They seemed to have tradition of always giving a piece of jewellery.

This studied unconcern is symptomatic of the Windsors and their financial attitude. 'Money is such a vulgar subject,' says Prince Charles, reflecting a widely held view among the royal family. Theirs is the 'dog lead' monetary philosophy, as in the now famous anecdote where the Queen once sent the young Charles searching the grounds of Sandringham after he lost a dog lead. Her ringing rebuke: 'Dog leads cost money' could serve as a symbol for the sturdy image of thrift and frugality the Windsors have portrayed. The Queen is untroubled by her portrait as an inordinately wealthy woman who still saves string and goes round turning off lights to save money. As the

In 1939, as Britain teetered on the brink of war, the royal family presented an assured picture of domestic calm and content.

Labour Prime Minister Clement Attlee once told the House of Commons: 'The royal family live simple lives, are approachable people, hard working and with no excess of luxury.' That show of domestic fidelity was captured by the royal photographer Sir Cecil Beaton in a series of charming studies of King George VI and his family during the Second World War.

This outward image of middle-class housekeeping is translated into the royal family's own behaviour towards money. Like many millionaires, they continually think they are hard up. For years Prince Philip religiously filled in his Vernon's football pools coupon telling anyone who would listen, 'If I hit the £500,000 ($850,000) jackpot at least I would have some money of my own.'

During a boar hunt on the Regensburg estate of Prince Thurn und Taxis in 1968, Prince Philip was astonished to find that a private family could still live in such a grandiose manner. He declared that the House of Windsor could not maintain such a lifestyle without handouts from the State. 'What do you expect,'

said his unsympathetic host. 'No workey, no money.'

The royal belief in their position of abject poverty is ingrained. Once, when the Queen was being driven in her Rolls-Royce to Windsor Castle, she spotted a greengrocer's shop on the Cromwell Road in London which had a large display of apples. As her limousine pulled away from the traffic lights she said to her chauffeur, Henry Purvey, 'Good gracious, is that the price of apples? Tell chef to take them off the menu.' On another occasion she spent hours with two Army officers and their metal detectors as they searched the grounds around Sandringham House for a tiny watch the Queen had lost while out walking.

These examples merely serve to illustrate that the royal family do not regard the standards and aspirations of the super rich as a bench-mark. Not for them the helicopter pads, the gold bath taps, and the swimming pools. Their belief in their relative economic deprivation is total. When Prince Charles decided to leave his temporary residence of Chevening he told Princess Michael of Kent that he had to spend

Balmoral, the effective family seat of the Windsors, bought by Queen Victoria in 1848.

too much time on road travel. 'Why don't you buy your own helicopter?' she innocently inquired. The Prince looked with blank incomprehension at his new relation.

As children, Prince Edward and Prince Andrew travelled to the nearby home of Lady Diana Spencer not only to enjoy nursery teas but because Sandringham was not equipped with a swimming pool. There was never any question of installing one on the royal estate because that would have meant change and any alteration to the royal routine produces the same effect on the family as sunlight on a vampire. Each autumn at Balmoral the Princess of Wales and the Duchess of York have to travel to a nearby hotel to enjoy a swim simply because the royal family refuse to change Queen Victoria's Highland home.

As one royal staff member commented, 'The royal family don't need to compete with anyone else. They don't need to social climb, they don't need to impress. They are number one and so they live by their own priorities. It is the little things that they value most.'

This belief in their own poverty does create problems, especially among new arrivals. In her early days Princess Michael of Kent spent much time and energy trying to convince the

Queen to put her on the Civil List and help defray her expenses. She and her husband are seen as the 'poor relations' of the royal family, making do with a butler, chauffeur, housekeeper, private secretary and clerical staff together with a country house, Nether Lypiatt, in Gloucestershire, a grace and favour home in Kensington Palace and, for a time, a hideaway on the Caribbean island of Antigua. In spite of their professed hardships, they are still millionaires in their own right as are all the other families – the Kents, the Gloucesters and the Ogilvies – within the Windsor dynasty. As the Princess once remarked to a friend who had spotted a newspaper report which said that Prince Michael earned a mere £20,000 ($34,000) from his City directorships, 'My dear, we couldn't support a bedsit on that.' However, that doesn't stop polite but remorseless letters from the royal bankers, Coutts and Company, reminding them about their overdraft.

It is the monarch herself who acts as banker to her immediate relations because the Queen is exempt from the tyranny of the Inland Revenue. She bought Gatcombe Park for Princess Anne as a wedding present, but provided the capital to buy further land, Aston Farm, thereby ensuring that property which is held in her name will not be taxed when it is passed down to future generations. However, Captain Mark Phillips has taken out a modest mortgage to improve his holdings.

Another insight of Royal business acumen comes from the American oil magnate, Dr Armand Hammer, who described a visit to Prince Charles' home at Highgrove in Gloucestershire:

After lunch he and I took a walk around his farm while his little boy Prince William scampered with us or was carried in his father's arms: 'I couldn't afford this farm myself,' he told me, 'but my mother lent me the money to buy it.'

The property itself is held in the name of the Duchy of Cornwall and will no doubt be passed down to Prince William when he becomes the Prince of Wales and entitled to the revenue from these extensive estates.

Private land is one thing, private expenditure on a wardrobe for public engagements is quite another. The royal family have made a very clear-sighted and necessary distinction

Princess Michael of Kent, at her Nether Lypiatt home, constantly complains that she and her husband Prince Michael are not on the Civil List.

between the money they spend from their Civil List on public duties and their own private fortune. There is very little crossover either way – as the Duchess of York discovered to her cost when she first joined the royal family.

Her overspending on clothes was such that she had to haggle with couturiers for substantial discounts. When she asked the designer Zandra Rhodes for financial preference in return for the resulting media coverage Miss Rhodes replied, 'Darling, I don't need the publicity.' For a young woman who only had a small private allowance, learning the rigid royal rules came as quite a shock. When she toured Canada in 1987 she discovered to her chagrin that the official Foreign Office clothing allowance for this overseas visit was only £2,000 ($3,400). As the royal family do not subsidize their public duties from their private purse the Duchess had to extend her stretched

overdraft. It became such a difficult subject that she had to find discreet ways to make money without seeming to exploit her royal position. Happily her own energetic efforts in writing two children's books on the adventures of a helicopter called Budgie went part of the way to solving her problems.

However, her husband the Duke of York is a millionaire in his own right. As with all her children, apart from Prince Charles, the Queen has established trusts worth around £1 million ($1.7 million) to enable them to live in the style in keeping with their station. They are discreetly administered by Earl Carnarvon, the Sovereign's racing manager and close friend, and her solicitor, Sir Matthew Farrer.

While the Queen is generous in a very traditional way – buying property and dispersing family jewels and heirlooms on marriage – she does not believe in extravagant running costs. So she vetoed the use of an expensive American interior design team, Hadley Parish, for the Duchess's new home at Sunninghill on the edge of Windsor Park, while happily paying for its construction.

As a former member of the Royal Household commented, 'You very quickly learn that while the royal family have everything, they have very

The future home of the Duke and Duchess of York, the first example of royal building in this reign.

basic needs. They keep everything far longer than any normal person because they like things to be familiar.'

So the clothes of Kings George V and VI are still kept in rooms at Buckingham Palace and no one in the family thought it strange that they should ask the tailor on board the royal yacht *Britannia* to alter a sports jacket worn by Prince Edward so that it would fit Princess Anne's son, Peter Phillips. Their indifference to the mechanics of money is perhaps epitomized by the fact that they never carry any. On royal tours there are often embarrassed fumblings when they spot something in a shop and wish to buy it. Foreign shopkeepers are bewildered when these people, who they know to be rich, have to wait for a bodyguard to pay for their purchases.

The Windsors have moved beyond the aspirations of wealth. What the average person would covet as magnificent possessions they view as necessary props. They subscribe to Frederick the Great's observation that 'a crown is just like a hat that lets in the rain'. So when Princess Margaret talks about the night of a Big Dressing – when all the royal ladies wear their finery – she does not discuss the relative cost of their tiaras but marvels at the fact that the Queen is the only person who can put hers on as she is walking downstairs.

'I think we ought to find something for the sapphires,' the Queen will say to her dresser, as though discussing an underused actor in the local repetory theatre.

Time and again in the papers and diaries of members of the royal family, references are made to the weight or discomfort of a crown – never to its worth or splendour. Thus the Princess of Wales complains that tiaras give her headaches, while King George V chaffed at the heaviness of the Indian Crown during the Delhi Durbar in 1911. This use of jewellery as a prop was epitomized at the investiture of Prince Charles as Prince of Wales in 1969 where the glowing orb on his crown was in fact a table tennis ball sprayed gold.

Indeed, Prince Charles personifies this outlook, perfectly reflecting the eighteenth-century poet and dramatist Oliver Goldsmith's verse: 'A man he was to all the country dear, and passing rich on £40 a year.' More prosaic-

ally one of his Household observed, 'If he has a clean £5 note for church on Sunday the man is happy.' However, that £5 note has first to be sprayed and ironed by his valet, neatly folded and then creased so that the Queen's head is facing outwards. Then the note is placed under his clove box – the Prince always chews a clove before every meal – prior to his departure for the morning service. Just as the Duke of Windsor would only allow the Duchess to use freshly minted money, so for the present Prince of Wales money is a prop in a ritual as elaborate as any Japanese tea ceremony.

The Prince of Wales' life is a routine where familiar objects provide reassurance in a changing world. When cleaners removed an ancient glass from his bathroom he wrote a piqued memo to his valet: 'I didn't mean you to remove that glass for my toothbrush. It was a *particularly* nice glass. *Please* bring it back. If they have removed it I shall be very angry indeed.' Like Queen Victoria he gives worth to an object — and for that matter an individual — because of its familiarity not its value. 'He hates change, everything is done how his mother or grandfather did things. The Prince is very

conscious of values, you never get the impression that he thinks he is well off, quite the opposite.' The former member of staff added, 'I remember that he was given a superb canteen of cutlery when he moved into High-grove. It arrived with its own modern but very tasteful stand. But the Prince didn't like it because it was new, it wasn't traditional.'

This attitude had its most eccentric display on a tour of Canada in the 1970s. During a visit to Winnipeg his valet had left behind a battered crocodile shoehorn and this omission was only discovered the following day when the royal

party were on Victoria Island on the Canadian west coast. The Prince was furious at the loss of his beloved shoehorn. Immediately the Winnipeg hotel was contacted, the errant shoehorn found and a Canadian air force jet despatched to fly the royal possession the 1,000 miles or so west. The plane was met at the airport by a police convoy and, with sirens wailing the shoehorn, lovingly wrapped in tissue paper, was delivered to the royal hotel. On another occasion, during an autumnal sojourn at Balmoral, the local greengrocers ran out of plums which the Prince eats for breakfast. The Prince, much put out by this interruption of his routine, rang his chef, Mervyn Wycherley, at Kensington Palace and ordered him to buy a box of Victoria plums and send them on the next royal flight to Scotland.

It may seem absurd but the Prince's almost other-worldly appreciation of monetary value serves as an emblem for the Windsors. For the royal family, worth does not correspond with value. Thus the Queen, on her annual cruise to the Western Isles, thought nothing of diverting the royal yacht *Britannia* to Holyhead so that she could post a letter, while the Princess of Wales followed her husband's example and during her first visit in 1983, had half a dozen hats flown out to New Zealand in the diplomatic bag because she didn't want to wear the same hat a second time.

In his own right Prince Charles is in the top ten of the richest individuals in Britain. In 1988 his publicly available accounts for the Duchy of Cornwall estates showed that he had an annual income of £1.9 million ($3.23 million), with share holdings of around £20 million ($34 million). In all his land holdings are worth £253 million ($430 million) according to current property prices.

Yet like the rest of his family, he feels no sense of extravagance or great wealth. His dressing gown, emblazoned with the Prince of Wales feathers, has been patched and mended. The Princess of Wales felt the rasp of his tongue when she bought him an expensive dinner jacket, while he will regularly send back lists of present suggestions from jewellers like Garrard or Collingwood because he feels they are too expensive. The Princess of Wales soon caught the mood, causing subdued guffaws when she announced in a television interview that she bought fish for her sons because it was cheaper. She, together with the Duke of York and Prince Edward, also bought 800 British Telecom shares when the company was privatized in order to benefit from the £18 ($30) voucher giving a discount on the quarterly bill. To date she has made £1,500 ($2,550) on her purchase.

Until his marriage, Prince Charles' financial life was a mess. Monthly balance sheets were only introduced when he invited a former shipmate, Michael Colbourne, to become the Comptroller of his Household. 'As long as he had enough to play polo, go fishing and skiing and look presentable, the Prince was unworried about his money,' recalls a former employee.

Marriage changed all that. During the preparations for the wedding at St Paul's Cathedral in 1981 there was consternation within the Prince's Household that he would be unable to afford the expenditure. 'Sums were worked out on the backs of envelopes, it was chaos,' remembers one of the combatants. The needs of the Princess of Wales and the Wales family forced the Duchy of Cornwall to become efficient.

Nevertheless, Charles does not take his wider financial status for granted. He has often discussed the privileges of his position in a world of want and hunger. 'Christ says: "Sell all you have and follow me." A lot of people would think I was quite mad and I'm not sure how much I could achieve after it,' he told one interviewer, articulating the traditional notions of *noblesse oblige*.

There is a continuing sense of stewardship within the Windsor dynasty, a custodial purpose not simply towards their own family but to the greater good of the nation. Time and again they have shown that they are prepared to defer immediate gratification for the sake of preserving the Windsor identity and through that a substantial national heritage. Even their sternest critics would never accuse the Windsors of salting away glittering treasures in shady places or shifting their cash to Swiss bank accounts. Royal munificence often goes unrecognized and unrecorded but it is responsible for sustaining a collection of treasures of unrivalled splendour and variety.

The Royal Stamp Collection lovingly built up by King George V, is the finest in the world while the royal jewels are breathtaking in their

A royal honeymoon on board the royal yacht
Britannia *includes a Royal Marine band.*

sensuous variety and dazzling glory. Corridor
after corridor of the various palaces are
decorated with examples of the finest works
of art man has created since the Renaissance
– hundreds of drawings by Leonardo da Vinci,
magnificent works by Rembrandt, Rubens,
Gainsborough and Raphael, including fifty-
three Canalettos. The catalogue of the royal
furniture alone runs to seventy-five thick
leather volumes. Windsor Castle houses a priceless collection of glass, exquisite china and
plate, fine bronzes and antique furniture while
the magnificent Royal Libraries and photo-
graphic collection have provided an invaluable
archive for scholars all over the world.

It is the historic quality of the royal collections which is so inspiring. Dr Armand
Hammer gave an American perspective when
he brought over a watercolourist, Bob Timberlake, to give Prince Charles some tuition. The
Prince invited Mr Timberlake, who had never
been out of his native North Carolina, to look
round the private apartments at Buckingham
Palace. As he admired the collections of
pictures and furniture he turned to Dr

Hammer and said, 'Where I come from, this is
what we call walking in tall cotton.'

The economics of scale do bring their own
problems. For example, a painting by the
European master Anthony Van Dyck stood for
years in the servants' corridor at Buckingham
Palace, neglected and undiscovered. It even
bore the water marks where it had been the
victim of the cleaner's floor mop. The picture
has since been restored to its proper glory.
It was sheer chance – and Queen Mary's
fastidious detective work – that rescued one of
Britain's most notable prehistoric antiquities
from oblivion. The Rillaton Cup, a very early
example of sheet gold work, was brought
to light after it had spent many years on
King George's V's dressing table holding his
collar studs. Similarly, a huge *art nouveau*
stained glass window commissioned by Queen
Alexandra was only rediscovered after the
present Queen initiated a search party of the
Buckingham Palace cellars. It is now delighting
visitors to Ely Cathedral.

However, there is a significant difference
between ownership and custodianship. This
is where many make mistaken assumptions
about the Queen and her private possessions
and hence the wealth of the Windsors. Most of

Prince Charles' private kingdom extends to the Duchy House on the remote Isles of Scilly.

the royal collections, certainly those built up prior to Queen Victoria's death in 1901, are held in trust for future generations and are, in the words of Lord Cobbold, 'inalienable'. Thus the royal palaces, the Queen's paintings, the State jewels, the Crown Estates, the royal collections of works of art dating back to King Charles I and beyond are under the Queen's stewardship. It is one of the outstanding features of her reign that the priceless heritage in her care has been so thoughtfully and methodically collated and displayed. As Sir Oliver Millar, the distinguished former Surveyor of the Queen's Pictures, observed during the Silver Jubilee celebrations, 'The Queen and the Duke of Edinburgh have done much to make the last twenty-five years the most lively in the history of the collection since the death of the Prince Consort in 1861.'

While there will be some necessary overlap, this book aims to examine the growth of the private royal collections and possessions as part of the story of the development of the House of Windsor from the accession of Queen Victoria in 1837. As Lord Cobbold, the former Lord

Chamberlain, told the Select Committee on the Civil List in 1971, 'The Queen and Prince Philip obviously own a considerable amount of furniture, pictures, jewellery, etc. in their own right, acquired by inheritance, gift or purchase. In addition, the Queen has her own private funds.'

Distinguishing between private dynastic property and possessions and that held in trust for the nation has many grey areas. As Mr Harold Brooks Baker, managing editor of *Burke's Peerage*, noted, 'If the Queen were to be banished into exile tomorrow there is not one man in the country who could say with absolute certainly what was owned by the royal family and by the nation.'

That view, while commonly held, would not find sympathy with the Queen nor, for that matter, her staff. The Queen is well aware of the distinction between her private and public possessions and has a remarkable capacity to request a long forgotten asset at awkward moments. As one long-serving member of staff observed, 'The Queen will often surprise us by asking for a table decoration that hasn't been used for twenty years or so. Yet she knows exactly where it is.' She gave a personal insight during her 1988 Christmas broadcast when she held a medieval Bible from the Royal Library at

The pink Fabergé Easter egg which is now worth at least £2 million ($3.4 million).

Windsor Castle and told her audience how much she enjoys viewing the possessions in her trust.

Certainly with the more valuable pieces, like the royal jewellery, the ground rules are scrupulously observed – in this reign at least. From time to time the Queen Mother enjoys wearing a Victorian diamond brooch from the State collection. However, her daughter is always quick to remark, 'Mummy knows that they are on loan and must be returned one day.'

While the present Queen has been a dutiful and imaginative steward of the 'inalienable' royal collections, there is no sense that she or her family are passive observers of the passing parade. Over the last thirty-six years she had done much to add to the wealth of the Windsor dynasty and its private possessions. The man who helped sustain the royal family's passion for the exotic confections of Carl Fabergé, Emanuel Snowman, once remarked that barely a week passed without him visiting Buckingham Palace to alter or redesign a piece of jewellery to the Queen's taste. His son, Kenneth, who has catalogued the private royal collection of Fabergé is probably as close to the monarch as any merchant ever can be – a sign of the Queen's discreet pursuit of *objects d'art*. She has maintained a tradition of collecting set by all the Queen Consorts in this century, most notably Queen Mary whose collections took three leather-bound volumes to catalogue. The majority has been bequeathed to the present Queen.

Queen Mary was as predatory as any shark, spotting treasures in private houses and antique shops and using all manner of persuasion to net her catch. During her stays at Sandringham, leading local families would hide their best china and antiques lest she chanced to visit.

The present Queen's interest is so quietly discerning it barely ripples the social waters. At the famous sale of the treasures of Lord Rosebery at Mentmore House in 1968 it was the Queen's agents, bidding secretly on her behalf, that set the pace for the prices of the extensive collections of porcelain. The present holders of the royal warrant for porcelain, Albert Amor, are guarded about the Queen's quiet hobby. 'You could find yourself in a lot of trouble asking about this. The royal family are very chary,' I was warned.

Princes William and Harry together with Peter Phillips play on the Merryweather fire engine at the Sandringham motor museum.

While the royal heritage of paintings is in the Queen's stewardship, this has not stopped her or her family building up a fascinating private collection from the Commonwealth, of modern artists like Edward Seago together with their own, not inconsiderable, efforts. Once again worth does not mean financial value. The gift of a painting from Sir Winston Churchill showing a scene of Wilton near Salisbury elicited the following charming response from the Queen. She wrote, 'Philip and I are so thrilled to have one of your pictures for our gallery — we do thank you most sincerely for this very kind gesture, and we do appreciate having such a delightful picture with a gloriously peaceful English summer scene.'

The Queen's passion for horse racing inspired her to make one of the few significant land purchases of her reign, the stud at West Ilsley in Berkshire. Typically, it was also a prudent business investment, turning a financial drain into a capital asset. Her substantial investment in bloodstock — she is one of the shrewdest judges of horse flesh in the world

— follows in the royal tradition set by King Edward VII. A statue of his legendary Derby winner, Persimmon, dominates the entrance to the royal stud at Sandringham. The Queen has yet to win that prestigious race just as the Queen Mother would love to triumph in the Grand National.

It is at Sandringham, too, that the royal collection of motor vehicles is maintained. The Queen is the only person who does not pay road tax or have number plates on her official limousines. This collection has never been a priority with any member of the royal family and yet it is still worth £250,000 ($425,000), underlining the fact that the Windsor heritage and position as the leading family in Britain plays such a crucial part in their dynastic splendour.

The Windsor fortune is unique, not deriving from business or land, but based on trust, tribute and tradition, leavened with constitutional privilege and possession. Theirs is an historic compact between nation and family, a union forged in the early hours of 20th June, 1837 when the Lord Chamberlain, Lord Conyngham, and the Archbishop of Canterbury arrived at Kensington Palace to inform a sleeping Princess Victoria of her destiny.

2
The Making of a Royal Dynasty

When the Princess of Wales is invested with the title of 'Sacred Majesty' and the Crown of State is gently placed on her head by the Archbishop of Canterbury, she will become the wealthiest Queen Consort in royal history.

Her eldest son, Prince William, the young schoolboy who is now photographed playing football with his friends, will inherit estates which will probably make him a billionaire in his own right. In the six generations since the accession of Queen Victoria in 1837 the transformation in the fortunes of the royal family has been truly remarkable.

When she was crowned Queen, Victoria inherited £50,000 ($250,000) worth of debts from her father, the Duke of Kent, and a monarchy noted more for its sexual and financial excesses than for its dignity and sense of duty. Yet just as the miserly King Henry VII sensibly dug the foundations of the Tudor dynasty, so Victoria's frugal nature was to be the lynchpin in the fortunes of the Windsors. Like her illustrious predecessor, she also had to contend with a son, the Prince of Wales, later King Edward VII, whose extravagant ways and dubious moral conduct made him the constant concern of the Cabinet and the butt of many a ribald pamphlet and music hall joke.

In a century which began with the sound of the guillotine still echoing through European palaces and which saw revolution, republicanism and Chartism — on oné occasion Victoria threatened to leave her troubled country and sail to Australia — the Queen adroitly maintained the monarchy, tenaciously guarding the remnants of its privileges and rights. That vigilance is no less eagle-eyed in the present reign. As the former Labour Prime Minister, now Lord Callaghan of Cardiff, says:

The Queen is always on the alert to make sure the monarchy is not being threatened at any point. She is quite right to follow every move for without her watchfulness the monarchy would not be in the strong position it is today.

When Princess Victoria accepted her heavy burden, she was the first to realize that the great tree of monarchy was ready to topple. A succession of kings had been treated with contempt by the aristocracy, indifference by the burgeoning middle class and derison by the mob. Its power, once absolute, was but a hollow echo of former days. Over the centuries monarchs had been hobbled by their responsibilities and now were shackled by their status.

Land, which had been the mainstay of the Crown's power, had been dispersed to pay for ruinous wars, a compliant nobility and, especially during the Stuart period, prodigal Court life. Even during the reign of Queen Elizabeth I, £120,000 ($600,000) worth of Crown lands and royal jewellery was sold in 1590 alone to maintain independence from Parliament.

It was an unequal struggle. In 1688 when King William III acceded to the throne — as ever in debt — Parliament passed the first Civil List Act. In 1697 the sum of £700,000 ($3.5 million) was set aside to pay for the whole machinery of civil government while the King was allowed to keep the revenues of his remaining land and assets.

This formula was unrealistic as government sucked in more funds while the English Court tried vainly to vie with the dazzling world of Louis XIV, the Sun King, and the excesses of the French Court at Versailles. Corruption was rife, the Royal Household was itself described as, 'a great nursery of indolence, parasites and courtiers'. Inevitably, both Queen Anne and King George I overspent their budget by £2.2 million ($11 million) over twenty-five years while King George II was forced to ask Parliament for an increase in the Civil List. With the accession of King George III in 1760 the

OPPOSITE: *A young Queen Victoria with her family, painted by John Calcott Horsley. Her good fortune, longevity and shrewd housekeeping marked a significant change from Hanoverian reigns.*

34

situation was reviewed once more, the power of the Crown being further eroded as a result of the Civil List Act of 1760 where the King's financial responsibilities were limited to providing for himself, his family, his Court, the civil service, the foreign service and the diplomatic corps. In return he surrendered the vast bulk of his Crown lands but retained his £800,000 ($4 million) a year grant which, together with rents from his remaining lands, brought his annual income to well over £1 million ($5 million).

Thus the constitutional precedent was established that the monarch's Civil List entitlement increased only marginally while its civic responsibilities were gradually removed.

While tradesmen and placemen waxed fat on the royal funds, politicians constantly railed against royal corruption. In 1782 the Tory philosopher and politician, Edmund Burke – who himself made £87,000 ($435,000) from the royal pocket – convinced Parliament to amend the original Civil List Act and further constrain the monarch's power. Four years later the King was £210,000 ($1,050,000) in debt while the Prince of Wales' wild extravagance was the talk of society. By the time he was twenty-two he was £400,000 ($2 million) in debt, the refurbishing of Carlton House contributing substantially to the 'torrent of expense'. His debts in 1787 included £29,000 ($145,000) on his stable account, a hobby he described as an 'almost divine amusement', before he got too heavy for the back of any normal horse. He was a preposterous dandy rouging his cheeks and corseting his bulk – twenty stone (280 lbs) at its peak – into expensive and gaudy clothes. He thought nothing of spending over £1,200 ($6,000) on a single outfit and during nine years of the Regency he bought no fewer than 500 shirts, grotesquely overspending on his clothing allowance.

By the time he became King in 1820 he was forced to surrender more Crown land to compensate Parliament for accepting further civil responsibility. His successor, William IV was as financially bankrupt as George IV. His personal debt was such – in 1818 he owed £56,000 ($280,000) – that he claimed that it was the reason why he did not wish to marry. It did not

The Coronation of Queen Victoria in 1837 marked the beginnings of the Windsor dynasty.

THE BUBBLERS MEDLEY, or a SKETCH of the TIMES
Being EUROPE'S MEMORIAL for the YEAR 1720.

Si Populus vult Decipi, Decipiatur

stop him from siring at least ten illegitimate children and sampling the diseased delights of numerous European brothels.

When he became King he divested himself of all remaining Crown lands, except the Duchies of Cornwall and Lancaster, as well as the responsibility for maintaining the Royal Palaces. In return, he received a substantially reduced Civil List of £510,000 ($2,550,000 expressly granted for the payment of such services and supplies as should 'affect the dignity and state of the Crown'.

Shadowing the shrinking of the monarch's civil authority, was the evolution of the notion of the King as a private person. During the Hanoverian period, the wrangling over numerous royal wills reveals this to have been a noisome progress, shrill with the sound of argument, anger and bitter advocacy.

BELOW: *Behind the pageantry of George IV's Coronation lay wrangling over his father's will.*

The dying words of King John Sobieski of Poland, who was asked to make a will on his deathbed, have particular relevance to the Hanoverian monarchs, 'The misfortune of royalty is that we are not obeyed when we are alive: and can it be expected we should be obeyed after we are dead?'

The will of George I, which contained a legacy to his mistress, the Duchess of Kendal, and a further substantial sum to his daughter, the Queen of Prussia, was burnt by his jealous son, George II. He made doubly sure by destroying the duplicate, excusing his vindictive behaviour on the pretext that his father had burnt two wills where he would have been the beneficiary.

However, in 1772, the Annual Register published another copy of George I's will where it was revealed that the late King had left £10,000 ($50,000) worth of his stock in the notorious South Sea Company to his mistress together with a further £12,986 2s 2d ($63,000) vested in the trust of the Prime Minister, Sir Robert Walpole. Significantly, alongside the will, was published a declaration from Sir Robert and

Queen Adelaide's jewellery, given to Queen Victoria, inspired a bitter family dispute.

eight learned judges as to the right of the King to dispose of his 'personalities' — that is his personal property, including his stocks and shares.

Although they established the principle of the monarch's possession of personal property, they decided that a King or Queen did not have the right to leave their private chattels by will. They ruled that their private goods automatically passed to the heir to the throne rather than to those the monarch favoured in a will.

George IV used this precedent with his family during the vicious struggle surrounding the wills of his parents, George III and Queen Charlotte. The only legatee of George III's first will, made and signed in 1770, was the Duke of York. It was based on the assumption that all the State property — the Crown Jewels, the palaces and land — automatically devolved upon his successor, George IV. The Duke of York was to receive around £20,000 ($100,000) together with the private family jewels. George IV vigorously and arrogantly contested the will, arguing that all the late King's possessions devolved upon him alone by virtue of legal precedent.

He bullied his brother in the same way over their mother's will. In the end the Duke of York withdrew from the family fight under protest, 'wishing to avoid any dispute or discussion of the subject begged to wash his hands of the whole matter'.

This acrimonious family feud saw a further twist when Queen Victoria came to the throne. She inherited many of the family jewels, including pearls from Queen Elizabeth of Bohemia, golden cutlery from George II, diamonds from George III and fashionable stones from her aunt, Queen Adelaide. Until her accession, the Hanoverian Kings had ruled both Britain and Hanover. However, in 1833 the German kingdom passed new laws which excluded women from the line of succession as long as a male descendant, however remote, survived. Queen Victoria's uncle, Ernest Augustus, Duke of Cumberland, became Elector of Hanover and duly demanded a portion of the jewels left by his brother on William IV's death, as part of his inheritance.

The break from Hanover was mirrored by the nature of Queen Victoria's personality. Piety, duty and a belief in family life marked a change from the profligacy and moral degeneracy of the previous reigns. The mad, the bad, and the sad days of the Hanoverian Georges were banished for good.

Queen Victoria's thrifty nature, a characteristic forged during her relatively impoverished childhood in the echoing and empty rooms of Kensington Palace, was crucial to her accumulation of both a personal fortune and, at times, public unpopularity. When she went to Westminster Abbey to celebrate her Golden Jubilee in 1887 she insisted on wearing a lace bonnet rather than a jewelled crown and luxurious velvet and ermine State robe. Lord Halifax declared that people wanted 'gilding for their money', while the Queen herself was deaf to the entreaties of her future Prime Minister, Lord Rosebery, that the Queen Empress was symbolized by a crown not a bonnet.

Queen Victoria's enduring fear of republicanism — the lurid stories of French aristocrats during the Revolution were the stuff of her childhood — made her err on the side of caution rather than conspicuous consumption.

OPPOSITE: *Queen Victoria wearing the diamond diadem worn by the Queen on British postage stamps. It was originally made for George IV.*

Her seven years' training in accountancy theory under the watchful eye of her tutor, Baroness Lehzen, neatly complemented a personality that was vigilant and obsessive yet impulsively generous.

Typically she set aside part of her Civil List allowance of £385,000 ($1,925,000) – a figure that remained static during her long reign – to pay off her father's debts. However, she performed the now traditional royal ritual of borrowing from the bankers, Coutts and Company. Within four months she was in credit and so she was to remain.

Her association with the Coutts family was always more than financial. Just as eighteen-year-old Princess Victoria was learning of her destiny, so Angela, the twenty-three-year-old daughter of Sir Francis Burdett MP and grand-daughter of Thomas Coutts the banker, was informed by lawyers that she was heiress to one of the greatest fortunes of the century. As the new Queen was considering her debts, so Angela Burdett-Coutts was assessing how to control an inheritance of £1,800,000 ($9 million). Contemporary newspaper accounts estimated her fortune most graphically. 'The weight in gold is 13 tons, 7 cwt, 3 qrts, 13 lbs and would require 107 men to carry it,' said one. As these two remarkable women endeavoured to live up to a destiny wrought by accident of birth, they were to forge a close friendship.

The Coutts family were familiar faces at court. At an early date the discretion and efficiency of Thomas Coutts earned him the trust and friendship of George III and in 1787 he was made a Gentleman of the King's Privy Chamber with direct access to the monarch. While the Prince Regent was a man of reckless and wilful habits, Coutts endeavoured to win him over using any manner of flattery to secure his favour. His success was complete when, like his father, George IV continued the habit of banking with Coutts. It is a tradition that is maintained to this day.

The Queen visited Angela Burdett-Coutts at her home in Stratton Street, enjoying the innocent proletarian pleasure of watching the passers by from the bay window. They corresponded through her lady-in-waiting, Lady Ely, mainly discussing the numerous charitable projects involving Miss Burdett-Coutts who was described as 'the Queen of the Poor'. Such was the Queen's respect for this demure,

Baroness Burdett-Coutts. Her generosity saved the Teck family from bankruptcy.

generous but strong-willed woman that in 1871 she became the first woman to be raised to the baronetage.

Her financial advice and assistance to the royal family was certainly a factor in her elevation. Her largesse was directed mainly at the impecunious figure of the Duchess of Teck, the mother of the future Queen Mary. She supported the Tecks during their frequent financial crises, often lending them her homes at Stratton Street or Holly Lodge in Highgate as well as £50,000 ($250,000) to pay off their numerous debts. It was indeed fortunate that the improvident rake, Prince Francis of Teck, a younger brother of Queen Mary, enjoyed the luxury of having the Baroness as a godparent although he did not profit as he had hoped from her will.

While the Queen benefitted greatly from the friendship of a wealthy heiress who always

Osborne House on the Isle of Wight. Queen Victoria loved the countryside and sea breezes.

referred to the monarch as an 'ever dear and cherished lady', the strict Teutonic tutelage of her Consort, Prince Albert, exerted a daily influence on the revival of royal fortunes.

Prince Albert of Saxe-Coburg and Gotha, from the German Duchy of Saxe-Coburg, was not universally popular. His marriage to Queen Victoria in 1840 was greeted by customary xenophobia. 'He came to take, for better or for worse, England's fat Queen and England's fatter purse,' ran one verse in the satirical magazine, *Punch*.

The strength of feeling against Prince Albert who, while not rich, was certainly well-to-do, was reflected in Parliament. While the Queen managed to secure a grant of £8,000 ($40,000) a year for her mother, the Duchess of Kent, she wished to invest in her 'dear Albert' the lavish annual sum of £100,000 ($500,000). However, the Liberal Prime Minister, Lord Melbourne,

convinced her that she should ask the country to supply half that amount. She and her Consort were much put out when, after vigorous debate in the House of Commons, that sum was slashed to £30,000 ($150,000), a sure sign of the uncertain status of the monarchy after a century of debauch. Albert remarked huffily that his reduced grant meant that he would be unable to patronize the arts as he would have wished.

As Prince Consort he constantly found his political moves blocked by suspicious politicians but his honest endeavours, particularly his masterly organization of the Great Exhibition at the Crystal Palace in 1851, eventually vindicated his reputation.

This restless, creative man was more influential and successful at Court where, under his methodical approach, the royal finances were finally organized. He was instrumental in reorganizing the farms on the Windsor estate, even designing the dairy which was a model of hygiene, decorated with Minton tiles and charming fountains. His efficiency was relentless, for example he allowed no visitor, 'however august and however spacious his bedroom', to have more than two candles to light his chamber.

The Prince's economies had the desired result. Income from the long settled heritage of the Duchy of Lancaster increased rapidly, from £26,000 ($130,000) in 1865 to £40,000 ($200,000) by 1872. Indeed, for the first time in years, the monarch was able to buy, rather than sell, land. The royal couple, who had a mutual love of the countryside and fresh air, bought Osborne House on the Isle of Wight for £26,000 ($130,000) in 1845, finding the mansion suitably remote from London. Originally they had hoped to buy nearby Norris Castle where the Queen had stayed as a child, but she admitted that they 'could not afford it'. However, Osborne was eminently agreeable. In her journal the Queen noted, 'It is impossible to imagine a prettier spot and we have a charming beach quite to ourselves – we can walk anywhere without being followed or mobbed.'

Three years later Balmoral in picturesque Deeside in Scotland was purchased for £31,500 ($157,500). Victoria expanded the estate con-

Queen Victoria at her Scottish home of Balmoral during a visit from the Russian Tsar and Tsarina (third from right).

siderably over the next twenty years with the purchase of adjoining forests and moors. While the Queen adored the new magnificent turreted castle they had built to replace the smaller house, most of her Household and Ministers detested it for its bleakness and remoteness. Lord Salisbury and Lord Rosebery recoiled in cosmopolitan horror when they viewed the endless tartan and antler furniture. 'I thought the drawing room at Osborne House was the ugliest in the world until I saw the one at Balmoral,' wrote Lord Rosebery.

While the taste of the royal couple was a matter of controversy, the reviving financial fortunes of the monarchy since their release from the heavy yoke of civil expenditure were irrefutable. The Victorian historian, Sir George Arthur, observed approvingly: 'Her affairs were so well managed that within 10 years she could pay a smart price for Osborne and Balmoral out of the savings of her income.'

As one of her Household noted, 'Economy with sufficiency has been the watchword of Her Majesty's career,' a point that was not lost on the Conservative Prime Minister, Sir Robert Peel, as he reflected on the State visits of Tsar Nicholas of Russia and King Louis-Philippe of France:

These visits, of necessity, created a considerable increase of expenditure but through that wise

system of economy which is the only source of true magnificence, Her Majesty was able to meet every charge . . . without adding one tittle to the burdens of the country.

Certainly fortune smiled on the righteous. In 1852, as the royal couple embarked on extensive plantings and alterations to their new estates, they received a truly remarkable legacy from an eccentric miser named John Camden Nield. He was the son of a well-to-do London goldsmith who had executed work for George III and spent his spare time in philanthropy, particularly in trying to help improve conditions in gaols. On his death he left his son a considerable fortune which Nield hoarded. When he died, aged seventy-two, it was discovered, to general astonishment, that he had left his fortune of £250,000 ($1.25 million) to 'Her Most Gracious Majesty, Queen Victoria, begging Her Majesty's most gracious acceptance of the same, for her sole use and benefit, and that of her heirs.' This generous gesture had widespread implications for the monarchy.

The Queen accepted the bequest, giving an annuity to a woman who had saved Nield's life when he threatened suicide. She also provided for his servants, increased the value of his bequests to his executors and built a chancel and window to his memory in his local church in North Marston, Buckinghamshire. This handsome legacy was invested for future generations and by the turn of the century was worth at least £1 million ($4.84 million).

While the Nield windfall provided independent financial security, the Queen was much exercised by the need for Parliament to provide for her growing family. In her journal of March 1862 she confided:

I feel very anxious about a provision for my Bertie and his wife, in the event of his marrying; a provision for my younger sons on their coming of age and marrying; and a provision for the younger children under age, in case of my death.

Suitable grants were made, although they didn't stop the Queen's second son, Prince Alfred, the Duke of Edinburgh, from supplementing his income by charging social climbers for the privilege of meeting members of his family. His services were not cheap. In Paris, for example, the going rate to meet his brother, the Prince of Wales, was 5 louis for a presentation and 50 louis for a luncheon.

The future Edward VII looking every inch the affluent society dandy.

While the Queen's influence within the Government preserved and expanded the financial integrity of the monarchy, Prince Albert's unstinting efforts rapidly improved the efficiency of existing estates. In between designing royal jewellery and medals he found time to revive the sluggish finances of the Duchy of Cornwall, the estate held in trust for the Prince of Wales. At the time of the Queen's accession, the estate was hopelessly mismanaged and it was only due to the Prince Consort's instinting efforts that his eldest son's heritage became a useful asset. By 1860 the Prince's accumulated income from the Duchy was £600,000 ($3 million) − 'a very large sum,' remarked Sir Charles Phipps, Keeper of the Privy Purse with characteristic understatement. It was easily enough to purchase the 20,000-acre estate of Sandringham in Norfolk for £220,000 ($1.1 million). The price excited local comment as, when the estate had been auctioned in 1836, it had only fetched £76,000 ($380,000).

OVERLEAF: *Sir Edwin Landseer's symbolic portrait of Queen Victoria and her retainer, John Brown.*

ABOVE: *Princess Alexandra's wedding procession in 1863 was the first manifestation of royal pageantry since Prince Albert's untimely death.*

Prince Albert hoped that the estate would save his son, with whom he enjoyed a brittle and distant relationship, from the distractions of London society and teach him to enjoy the sober pleasures of a healthy, country life. As negotiations reached a crucial stage, Prince Albert contracted typhoid fever, dying at the early age of forty-two on 14th December, 1861.

As the Queen nursed her grief it seemed that the sterling efforts of her beloved husband would be frittered away as the Prince of Wales embarked on a scale of extravagance that would have earned him the applause of the notorious King George IV.

With Prince Albert's death, too, the aggressive expansion and streamlining of the royal assets effectively ceased. Nothing that was his was moved after his death. His walking sticks, his despatch boxes, his paper weights, everything was preserved. Every night before dinner water was poured into his basin by a servant while the Queen, who was always to wear the

OPPOSITE: *The royal mausoleum at Frogmore built by Queen Victoria for her Consort, Prince Albert.*

black of mourning, clasped his nightclothes to her when she retired to bed. She spent £200,000 ($1 million) from the £500,000 ($2.5 million) Prince Albert left her in his will on the Royal Mausoleum at Frogmore. The Prince of Wales contributed a further £10,000 ($50,000) from his own funds.

Full Court life was effectively curtailed even though the Queen continued to draw the Civil List and her revenue from the Duchy of Lancaster. She stayed in Buckingham Palace for only eight nights a year – one wag hung a sign on the gates offering the mansion for sale – yet she insisted on maintaining her rights of passage over Hyde Park. No traffic was allowed through the royal parks nor down Constitution Hill until the early 1880s and then subject to the provision that no traffic must pass north of Buckingham Palace when she was in residence.

The nation grew tired of her morbid grief for her husband and, at a time when Britain was celebrating its industrial glory and vision of empire, demanded a figurehead to reflect that pride. Republicanism grew apace especially when it was pointed out that the Civil List was thirty times the size of the American President's salary. In 1871 Simon Templar's pamphlet *What does She do With It?* noted that her income was tax free and that only a small

ABOVE: *Marlborough House, the home of the future Edward VII, was the glamorous hub of society life.*

part went to maintain the dignity of the Crown. In Parliament, the Radical Liberal Charles Dilke proposed a motion to inquire into her finances and to reform the Civil List, arguing that the Queen's continued seclusion was a 'malversion' of public funds. The Queen wrote indignantly to her Prime Minister, William Gladstone, denying the charges that she did not pay income tax. She complained, 'Gross misstatements and fabrications, injurious to the credibility of the Queen, and injurious to the monarchy remain unnoticed and uncontradicted.' The Prime Minister was forced to remind her that she did escape this unpopular tax, which was introduced in 1842 by Peel as a temporary measure.

However Dilke was soundly defeated, partly due to a wave of sympathy for the maligned Queen who had been seriously unwell. That sympathy became universal when the Prince of Wales narrowly escaped death from typhoid fever – the same disease that had carried off his father exactly ten years earlier. His excesses were forgiven by his mother and the nation as he slowly recovered. Yet while the doctors cured his disease, he was firmly smitten by the Hanoverian virus of conspicuous consumption.

The first manifestation of this came with his betrothal to the beautiful Princess Alexandra of Denmark. He sent her £3,000 ($15,000) for her trousseau and £15,000 ($75,000) in jewels which included a complete set of diamonds and pearls. The wedding ring was set with six precious stones, the initials of the gems spelling 'Bertie'. His future bride was granted £10,000 ($50,000) as pin money while the Danish people presented her with 100,000 kroner, known as the People's Dowry. The money went to help poor Danish women. Her father, King Christian, gave her a necklace containing 2,000 brilliants and 118 pearls.

The Prince's lavishness was certainly not constrained by his marriage. During the 1860s he overspent on his Duchy of Cornwall income by as much as £20,000 ($100,000) a year, drawing heavily on his capital to pay off his gambling losses. He lost £239 ($1,195) in two nights during March 1865 and £700 ($3,500) on two successive nights in August 1867 – more than a worker in the 'satanic mills' that

OPPOSITE: *The sombre dress of court mourning added to Princess Alexandra's bejewelled dignity.*

fuelled the nation's wealth would earn in a lifetime. In 1869 the Prince was forced to sell his Windsor Harriers pack of foxhounds to save £2,000 ($10,000) even though hunting was his passion. (He once chased a deer through the streets of London before cornering and killing it in the goods yard at Paddington Station.)

His London home was established at Marlborough House, which thanks to the earlier efforts of his father had been refurbished by the Government and held in trust until the Prince came of age. Over 100 staff were on call who would all be required when the Wales hosted a ball, as in 1872, for example, when the Prince held a fancy dress ball for 1,400 guests. The Prince came as King Charles I, covered in diamonds and wearing a wig, while guests enjoyed supper in two huge red marquees hung with priceless tapestries. It was, remarked Disraeli, 'gorgeous, brilliant, fantastic'.

His social round was as brilliant as it was expensive. Grouse shooting in Scotland, sailing at Cowes and in London what he described as, 'the gaieties and frivolities of the great city'. He rented a house in Chiswick from the Duke of Devonshire to pleasure his mistresses, enjoyed baccarat at Marlborough House and watched music hall acts from behind a screened box. At one wild party he was carried around the house in a sedan chair until a pole broke and sent him tumbling to the ground. On a late night visit to a gambling den, the Archduke Rudolf of Austria ordered the waiters out of the room as 'they must not see their future King making such a fool of himself', and he once danced the can-can with the Duchess of Manchester. He was involved in the sensational Mordaunt divorce case and the Tranby Croft gambling scandal, surviving both with his reputation, such as it was, intact.

His spending was so high that friends were driven into bankruptcy in vain attempts to maintain his luxurious standards. It was widely rumoured that Lord Suffield burned down half his country seat in a desperate attempt to stop 'Bertie' from visiting him.

Abroad he travelled in style. On a journey down the Nile to view work on the Suez Canal, the Prince's luxury barge was accompanied by six blue and gold steamers, each of which had a barge full of supplies. One carried a cargo of 3,000 bottles of champagne, 4,000 bottles of claret, 10,000 pints of beer, together with four French chefs.

As he sat shaded from the Mediterranean sun, he received a letter from his mother which enscapsulated the divide, both moral and financial, that lay between them:

I hope dear Alix will not spend much on dress at Paris. There is, besides, a very strong feeling against the luxuriousness, extravagance and frivolity of Society; and everyone points to my simplicity. I am most anxious that every possible discouragement should be given to what, in these radical days, added to the many scandalous stories current in Society . . . reminds me of the Aristocracy before the French Revolution . . .

In 1874 while the Prince was in Baden taking the waters and gambling, rumours swept through Society that he was £600,000 ($3 million) in debt. The Queen's private secretary, Henry Ponsonby, prompted by the irate monarch, staunchly defended the future King. In a letter to Sir Arthur Helps he wrote in vexed tones:

Paragraphs have been lately appearing about the Prince of Wales's debts. Mr P. A. Taylor has written a letter to his constitutents about them and the *World* has published three leading articles stating that His Royal Highness owed £600,000 [$3 million], that he applied to Mr Gladstone to bring the matter before Parliament, and that he refused, that Mr Disraeli was to be asked to do so, and finally that the Queen has paid off these debts.

There is not a word of truth in any of the above statements.

If the Prince of Wales at any time exceeds his annual income on account of his building operations or from other similar causes, he has met the extra call by falling back on his capital. But these excesses of expenditure over income have been very trifling. It is utterly untrue that he is in debt.

Loyalty may have triumphed over truth. Certainly as he approached middle age, the Prince felt stretched, cultivating the previously hostile Dilke and Radical Liberal Joseph Chamberlain as he tried to woo Parliament into a vote of funds for his five children. In the event the Prince of Wales was awarded a capital sum of £60,000 ($300,000) for his own use, together with a further £36,000 ($180,000) to assign to his children as he thought fit. His total income was now £150,000 ($750,000) and the vote established the principle of the government's obligation to provide for the children of the sovereign's eldest son. However, the

protests at the measure were so vociferous –
critics claimed the Prince would use the money
to pay off his gambling debts – that Queen
Victoria hastily withdrew a suggestion that the
State should provide for the children of her
other sons.

While the Prince attempted to place his
wayward affairs on a sound footing, rumours
persisted that his expenditure continued to be
excessive. During a visit to Paris, the Prince's
hotel appeared to be ringed by touts and
suspect moneylenders. The British Ambassa-
dor to Paris, Lord Lytton, told the Prime
Minister, Lord Salisbury, that he had initiated
private inquiries through the head of the
French police 'with a view to the protection
of H.R.H. from the abuse of his name and
position'. Lytton's motive was to scotch persis-
tent reports that the Prince of Wales owed large
sums to unscrupulous moneylenders.

Yet at the very time that the Prince was
judged to be deeply in debt, he was planning a
major excursion into the expensive world of
'J-class' yacht racing. In 1893 he paid £9,000
($45,000) for the elegant cutter, *Britannia*,
and embarked on a highly successful career in
yacht racing.

Nonetheless, questions continued to be
asked with attention focussing on the dubious
characters he admitted into his circle. The
questionable sale of honours caused much
disquiet in Society. Lord Suffield, a friend of the
Prince of Wales, was offered a sea wall round
his country estate by one man and £250,000
($1,250,000) by another in return for a peerage.
Gladstone's secretary, Edward Hamilton,
referred to four men who had been recommended for baronetcies and the Prince of
Wales' dubious role in the affair. He noted in
his journal:

It is perhaps hardly fair to say so but these recommendations have rather an ugly look about them. A
respectable clergyman (the Rev. H.W. Bellairs) wrote
not long since to say that he was in possession of
information to which he could swear, that there
were certain persons scheming for hereditary
honours, and bribes to people in very high life . . .
that a gentleman told him that he had been offered
a baronetcy by the Prince of Wales . . . on condition
that he would pay £70,000 ($350,000) to the Prince's
agent on receiving the title.

Only one of the four men recommended by the
Prince was 'known to ordinary fame', Hamilton

*A jaunty Edward VII, immaculate as always, on
board his beloved 'J-Class' yacht* Britannia *which
out-classed most of her rivals.*

added. This was a rich building contractor,
C. J. Freake, and for him a knighthood would
have been quite sufficient. Yet the Prince
'persistently and somewhat questionably (if not
fishily)' pressed Freake's name upon Gladstone.

His friendships flourished with the dissolute
and dissipated. The Marquis of Waterford
eloped with the wife of his best friend, Lord
William d'Earesby, Joint Hereditary Grand
Chamberlain of England, and stole thousands
of pounds from his mistress before running off
with her maid, while the heir to Lord Winchlow
died in a brothel. Another lord married a
bigamist inspiring *The Times* to comment:
'When a peer of high rank drags his dignity in
the dirt . . . he stains his order.'

It was not morality but birth which most
vexed the Queen and her friends as they
observed the Prince's friends. The very men
who helped save the Prince from financial
ruin were those most abhorred by the Court.

Lady Warwick said, 'We resented the introduction of the Jews into the social set of the Prince of Wales, not because we disliked them individually but because they had brains and understood finance. As a class we do not like brains. As for money our only understanding of it lay in the spending, not in the making of it.'

That the Prince should entertain Baron Hirsch, the Rothschilds, Louis Bischoffsheim, the Sassoons, Sir Blundell Maple, the furniture king, Sir Thomas Lipton, the food baron, and Sir Ernest Cassel, horrified Society. Even *The Times* objected to his hobnobbing with 'American cattle men and prize fighters', and the Queen refused to meet Hirsch even though he was the Prince's senior financial advisor. These self-made men formed a tightly knit and powerful group which stayed with him during his transition from monarch-in-waiting to King Emperor.

The most important of these friendships was that of the German Jewish financier, Sir Ernest Cassel. He was Hirsch's executor and when he died in 1896, Cassel easily slipped into his

Edward VII's financial advisor, Sir Ernest Cassel. His investments ensured royal solvency.

shoes as the Prince's financial advisor and closest confidant. Such was his hold over the King that when Edward VII asked the Portuguese diplomat, the Marquess de Soveral, if he had seen Oscar Wilde's play *The Importance of Being Earnest*, the diplomat replied archly, 'No Sire, but I have seen the importance of being Ernest Cassel.' The *bon mot* gained wide currency as did the nickname 'Windsor Cassel'.

Born in Cologne in 1852 into an insignificant Jewish family, he left school at fourteen to become a clerk before emigrating to London as the manager of the international finance house of Bischoffsheim and Goldsmidt. Tough, ruthless, but scrupulously honest, he made his fortune by shrewd investment in the railways of the New World and Scandinavia. At the height of his wealth he was said to have made £1 million ($4.84 million) in a day's trading on the Stock Exchange.

With single-minded resolve he taught himself the necessary social graces of riding and shooting while investing heavily in the breeding and racing of horses. It was at a race meeting that Cassel was introduced to the Prince of Wales. They shared a distinct physical resemblance but, on the surface, little else. As Cassel's biographer, Brian Connel, observed:

The Prince, extravagant by nature, addicted to forms of expenditure which required in a gentleman of honour the ability to produce at short notice large sums in cash, could use to good purpose the advice concerning his investments and private property of a financial expert of proven judgement and integrity. It is difficult to see any other basis for their ripening acquaintance.' Lady Oxford said of him, 'A man of natural authority who from humble beginnings became a financier of wealth and importance. He had no small talk and disliked gossip; he was dignified, autocratic and wise.

He was also obsessed with place and position, the summit of his ambition was to see the King agree to be the godparent to his granddaughter Edwina, later Countess Mountbatten of Burma. In 1908 he demanded the honour of Grand Cross Order of the Bath in return for acceding to the Foreign Secretary's request to loan the State Bank of Morocco £500,000 ($2.42 million). Rumours that he paid off the future King's gambling debts abounded and in a

OPPOSITE: *George V continued his father's passion for the expensive world of big yacht racing.*

N. Sotheby Pitcher

His Majesty's yacht "Britannia"
Turning   at Cowes 1913

climate where the Prince of Wales was implicated in the sale of honours it may well have been that in the early days of their friendship there was the classic trade between the upwardly mobile Cassel and the man who was the effective fountainhead of social standing. He was made a Privy Councillor and his philanthropy – he gave away £2 million ($9.7 million) of his fortune – earned him virtually every decoration at the King's disposal, including the Grand Cross of the Victorian Order.

While their personal friendship flowered, Cassel's growing links with Court saw him firmly entrenched among the royal circle, acting as financial adviser and arbiter. His correspondence with the King and his advisors provides a fascinating insight into the esteem in which he was held.

Just a few weeks after Queen Victoria's death in January 1901, the new King was considering his financial future. In March he deposited funds with Cassel, a trust his friend conscientiously observed:

I hereby acknowledge from His Majesty the King the sum of £20,685 ($100,000). This sum is deposited with me for the purpose of being invested. The records of this and any further transactions I may make on behalf of His Majesty will be kept in an account on my books this day entitled: Special AA Account.

The full fruits of this special account will never be known as the papers were deposited with his will and are no longer available. However, the King reaped a quick harvest. In November 1902, he wrote from Sandringham thanking Cassel for 'a cheque for £10,000 ($48,400) worth of the money you kindly invested for me.

While much correspondence concerned their mutual interest in shooting and horse-racing, from time to time a business note was introduced. In February 1903, Cassel wrote to the King from his home in Grosvenor Square:

I was very sorry to hear of Your Majesty's indisposition and I venture to send my best wishes for a speedy recovery. Referring to our conversation about Your Majesty's investments I have the honour to report that there is upwards of £30,000 ($145,200) available.

As one biographer, Sir Philip Magnus, has noted, 'By 1907 King Edward VII was relieved of encumbrances and was enabled to enjoy the whole of his income during the last three years of his life.'

When King George V ascended to the throne, the reins of royal finance once again returned to the old school. The autocratic Lord Revelstoke, the Eton and Cambridge educated senior partner at Baring Brothers, was probably the most influential banker in the City, bringing his financial acumen to bear on the King's affairs. He was the Receiver-General of the Duchy of Cornwall from 1908 until his death in 1929. A measure of his closeness to the Crown was that when the King, himself recovering from illness at Bognor Regis, was told of Revelstoke's death he admitted to his successor, Sir Edward Peacock, 'I feel like dying too'.

However, while Lord Revelstoke directed the King's affairs, Cassel was not left completely out in the cold. Even during the First World War when Sir Ernest's German background made him a social outcast, George V entrusted him with his investments, allowing him to build up a share portfolio outside Britain. In August 1915, the King wrote to him from Windsor Castle:

I am glad to hear what you tell me about the Oil Certificates and that you have been able to realise some of them at a small profit. It is indeed a blessing that most of your fortune is invested in America and is therefore safe.

Thank God I am keeping well but I am beginning to feel the strain of this terrible war, I fear the end may be a long way off.

Nevertheless, the period of Cassel's greatest influence was during Edward VII's ascendancy, a fact that the King's friends and advisors were quick to take advantage of. Even the King's mistress, Mrs Alice Keppel, benefitted from his sagacity with 'happy and fortunate results'. In 1906, for example, he received a fulsome letter from the King's private secretary, Lord Knollys, giving details of a share deal with Sir Thomas Lipton which had gone wrong and could bring potential friction with the King:

I know no one to whom I could refer such a question than to you and whatever your advice may be I shall follow it with a feeling of gratitude to you for having given it to me. I should add that I only have 1,000 shares as 1,000 out of the 2,000 belongs to the King.

OPPOSITE: *Edward VII was a participant in the labyrinthine rituals of the secretive Freemasons.*

Edward VII's long-time mistress, Mrs Alice Keppel. Her position at Court was so secure that Ernest Cassel made investments on her behalf.

In a pleading postscript he added:

I think it would be better that I should not mention the Lipton affair to the King until I have had your answer.

While Lord Knollys was technically in control of the King's finances, it is clear that he privately bowed to Cassel's wisdom. Personal rapacity and furtive secrecy combined to unsettle the judgement of the royal advisors in their efforts to make a killing on the Stock Market. The uncertain Knollys and dubious Lord Farquhar, Master of the Household, were implicated in shady dealings in Siberian mining shares, while the King strove to mask his own activities by using trusted friends as named investors. However, where he strayed from the course recommended by Cassel he took a tumble.

One of his letters, written from Marlborough House in November 1899 – a month after the start of the war against South Africa – and embossed with a large *ICH DIEN* on the red seal closing the envelope, ran as follows:

My Dear Mrs Paget,
Many thanks for your letter received this morning . . . I am very grateful for all you tell me about Mr. K . . . and you will naturally understand that knowing him so slightly I should hardly like being under any obligations to him. Still, one cannot be too grateful to him for his good advice – especially in these 'hard times!'
As he suggested 'Rands', would you kindly purchase them in your name which you yourself suggest, so that my name does not appear in any way. I leave it also to you the amount of stock that should be purchased, as you have a far better head for those things than I have.

Shares in East Rands, Rand Mines and Rand Victoria all fell in value as the war became increasingly bitter although his misguided investment during wartime shows a want of judgement in a man who not many years afterwards was hailed as a European statesman. His attitude contrasts vividly with that of Queen Victoria who daily agonized over the growing losses and, a month after her son bought his South African shares, was telling the Prime Minister, Arthur Balfour, 'We are not interested in the possibilities of defeat; they do not exist.'

The family interest in South Africa was further complicated by the fact that Edward

VII's son-in-law, the Duke of Fife, was vice-chairman of the British South Africa Company. An added twist to the saga is that on his sixty-sixth birthday the burghers of the Transvaal gave the King the fabulous Cullinan diamond. Was his unwitting financial support for the Boers a factor?

While the Prince talked about 'hard times' it is worth remembering the splendid heritage to which he was heir. During Queen Victoria's reign, tribute cascaded on the royal family on a scale hitherto unimagined. Royal weddings were glittering showpieces where foreign royalty vied with one another in the lavishness of their gifts, while the daily glamour of their lives was celebrated throughout the empire. When Edward became King he employed fifty kitchen staff alone while the royal chef, Monsieur Menager, followed the King on his visits to ensure that the royal palate was never deprived.

A description of the impressive Gold Pantry at Windsor Castle by a Victorian servant, published in 1897, gives an indication of the wealth at the command of the royal family.

The royal group after lunch during a shoot at Sandringham. The king's mistress, Mrs Keppel, wearing a black veil, stands behind her lover.

You start to separate the centrepieces from amid clusters of candelabra, a continuous background of gold sconces, rose water dishes, salvers and plaques or endless piles of gold dinner plates and dishes. To reach 50 or 60 is quickly done, but then you lose count . . . though much of the gold and silver plate at Windsor is Crown property, the Queen can claim nearly half a million pounds' worth as her own.

Flagons from the Spanish Armada, a gold dinner service for 140, and shelves glowing with their load of solid silver candlesticks formed part of a display which has changed little to this day.

Queen Victoria, who had commended the 'simplicity' of her life to the Prince of Wales, made daily if prosaic use of this heritage as her private secretary Henry Ponsonby noted:

I remember being sent for at Windsor while she was having breakfast. Everything on the table was gold, which seemed all in the picture, and she was eating a boiled egg in a gold egg cup with a gold spoon. Two Indian Khitmagars in scarlet and gold remained motionless behind her chair, while outside a page and a Scotchman in a kilt waited till she rang.

Death did not bring an end to her authority. She left detailed instructions about her funeral arrangements, even down to the music, with

Part of the fabulous collection of gold plate held in the vaults at Windsor Castle. It is occasionally used at State banquets.

her executors, Princess Beatrice and the Duke of Connaught. The Prince of Wales and Princess Beatrice had two papers addressed jointly to them and dated 25th October 1897 and 21st January 1898 where she dispersed the fortune accumulated over sixty-four years.

Her principal estates of Balmoral, Sandringham and Osborne together with the 'important' family jewels were left to the new King and his Consort, Queen Alexandra. The bulk of her fortune, estimated at £4 million ($20 million), was distributed among her surviving children and grandchildren. As with previous royal wills, the intentions of the deceased were promptly ignored. The Queen had wanted her home on the Isle of Wight to remain as a shrine to Prince Albert, intending too that her beloved Balmoral would still reflect the memory of her faithful servant, John Brown.

The King, however, took perverse pleasure in smashing every statue and ornament celebrating the plain-speaking Brown. A similar fate faced Osborne. As Prince of Wales he had grown to hate it and often tried to hide behind the marble pillars in the drawing-room to avoid making polite conversation on topics set by the Queen. After consulting lawyers – and his own conscience over breaking the terms of his mother's will – he was able to dispose of the country retreat as a Royal Navy training college and hospital for sick Naval officers. Only the central pavilion remained a family shrine.

Edward VII's short reign heralded a new age for the monarchy as well as the country. When giving evidence to a Parliamentary Select Committee on the King's finances, his private secretary Lord Knollys was able to boast, 'For the first time in English history, the heir apparent comes forward to claim his right to the throne unencumbered by a single penny of debt.' The Chancellor of the Exchequer raised the royal income from £385,000 ($1,925,000), set in 1837, to £470,000 ($2,274,800) together with an increase in the annuity of Queen Alexandra and a grant to the Prince of Wales of £90,000 ($435,600) a year.

On his own death in 1910, there was confusion over the terms of the King's will. It centred around the question of which jewellery belonged to the Crown and which was the King's private property. According to the King's lawyers it had not been his intention to leave

As Edward VII lay dying, Queen Alexandra returned this Fabergé cigarette case to Mrs Keppel which she had discreetly given to her royal lover.

Queen Alexandra all 'his jewels, ornaments, articles of Art or vertu, curiosities and other chattels', but because he did not know which jewellery she wanted to keep, he left her to make the final choice. She had no time or respect for legal technicalities and herself died intestate in 1925.

The two pieces which gave rise to most difficulty were King Edward's Garter Star and the famous diamond circlet − 'the lovely little crown' as Queen Mary's aunt, the Grand Duchess Augusta, described it − which was usually worn by Queen Alexandra at the State Opening of Parliament. A compromise was reached with Queen Alexandra. She would retain the Garter insignia for her lifetime while the diamond crown was returned to Queen Mary for the 1911 Opening of Parliament.

There may have been confusion over the division of the jewellery, but there was no doubt that the late King left his successor, George V, a rich man. While he cultivated an image of suburban simplicity − reinforcing collar studs with gold to make them last and rebristling his hair brushes − he was a man who lived in abundance, if not opulence. As his eldest son, the future King Edward VIII, observed:

I knew no one who liked his comforts more, save perhaps myself. Everything about him was always of the best − his clothes, his fine hammer guns by Purdey, his food, his stationery, his cigarette cases by Fabergé . . . the presents he gave to his friends.

George V continued his father's tradition of yacht racing and indulged his wife's passion for acquiring jewellery, particularly from the Romanov and other collections.

Even as Prince of Wales, George had quietly spent large sums of money on the main passion of his life, stamp collecting. In 1882, for example, when his father was attempting to influence Parliament to increase the royal grant, he bought a collection for £3,000 ($15,000), while eight years later he purchased the Caillebott collection for £5,000 ($25,000) − these prices in an age where a police officer earned 19 shillings a week. By the end of the First World War he had privately bought twenty-two individual collections and always took particular delight in pointing out to visitors where he had purchased a bargain.

Bejewelled Indian Maharajahs pay homage to George V on the lawn of Buckingham Palace shortly before his Coronation in 1911.

In 1904 he paid the unheard of sum of £1,450 ($7,018) for a rare Mauritian stamp which a Hampstead schoolboy had found by chance in his own collection. He enjoyed telling the story of how a royal courtier, unaware as to the identity of the purchaser, had told the King, 'This is all very interesting but who was the unmentionable fool who paid £1,450 for what is after all just a piece of paper?' The King replied, 'I was.'

His absorption in his collection was legendary and he would spend three afternoons a week on his hobby. Before he died he had painstakingly amassed a priceless collection that ran to 365 red leather-bound volumes.

This sedentary hobby combined with a family life of probity and quiet domesticity seemed in keeping with an age recovering from a cataclysmic war and a world-wide depression. Queen Mary, dignified, dedicated and distant, symbolized the popular image of modern monarchy. She had known the humiliation of genteel poverty and never forgot its salutary lessons. She refused to pay more than 25 guineas for a dress and constantly chided her mother-in-law, Queen Alexandra, about her extravagance, noting with alarm the 'hundreds of thousands of pounds' she lavished on war charities. Most galling was her spending on Sandringham – the home left to Queen

In 1904 George V paid the unheard-of sum of £1,450 ($7,018) for a rare Mauritian 2d stamp discovered in a schoolboy's collection.

Alexandra in Edward VII's will. When Queen Mary suggested that she might save money by ordering fewer cut flowers, Queen Alexandra curtly replied, 'I do like a lot of lovely flowers about the house and in my rooms.' She confided in Arthur Davidson, an old friend of the late King, 'If I get into debt they can pay.' She even hid £1,000 ($4,340) in a sofa at Sandringham so that her private secretary could not prevent her from giving to her favourite charities.

Queen Mary's impecunious younger brother, Prince Francis of Teck, was even more difficult to handle. His behaviour was the talk of the royal circle. In her memoirs Princess Alice, Countess of Athlone, reflected:

From boyhood Frank had always been a family problem. He had been expelled from Wellington College for throwing his housemaster over a hedge to win a bet. All his life he was an incorrigible gambler . . . as he grew up this gambling vice became worse.

In 1895 he lost £10,000 ($50,000) – a truly enormous sum – at Punchestown race course in Ireland and his sister, Princess May, and by then, the Duchess of York had to rescue her dissolute brother to avoid a public scandal.

He was banished to India for several years only to become entangled with an older married woman, Lady Constance Kilmorey, who was also, at one time, mistress of the Prince of Wales. As a foolhardy token of his regard he sent her the famous Cambridge emeralds which were part of the Teck family heirlooms. This rash act caused a serious breach between brother and sister and when he died suddenly in 1910, Queen Mary immediately sent a member of the Royal Household to Lady Kilmorey to request their return. Contemporary gossip claimed that she was given an emerald brooch as the price for her silence.

More intriguing was the secrecy surrounding Prince Frank's will. While the basic details were published – he left an estate of the gross value of £23,154 ($112,065) – the President of the Probate Division of the High Court ordered that probate be granted to his two brothers but that a copy of the will and codicil should not be

OPPOSITE: *Princess May of Teck with her family. This photo, taken in 1884, shows the future Queen with her mother and brothers, Princes Adolphus, Francis and Alexander.*

annexed. Effectively this meant that Prince Frank's will was 'sealed', and could not, as is customary, be examined by the public. Until that time every royal will had been open to historians and other interested parties. Why was a minor member of the royal family accorded such special treatment? The most likely explanation is that the emeralds had been willed to his lover in contravention of a family understanding to pass them on to Queen Mary. Thus any public embarrassment was neatly avoided and the family name remained unsullied.

This episode highlights two fascinating themes of the Windsor story. Firstly, the legal order made explicit the notion that the royal family were now a private family performing unique public duties which demanded special privileges rather than, as in the past, public figures whose lives were technically accessible to all.

Secondly, while Queen Mary's love of jewellery and possessions was legendary, a deeper sense of family heritage was revealed. Like Queen Victoria, Queen Mary had an innate feeling for the royal family and its historic destiny. Her voracious appetite for collecting furniture and *objets d'art* was complemented by her desire to search out anything that illuminated the story of the House of Windsor. She spent years ferreting out long-lost heirlooms or objects with a royal connection, embarking on long correspondence with owners, many of whom lived abroad. Her eldest son recalled in his memoirs,

This quest, pursued with pertinacity and diligence, continued throughout her lifetime, providing her with unending interest and satisfaction. 'You remember those missing candlesticks from the Cumberland silver,' she would ask. Then without waiting for an answer she would continue delightedly. 'Where do you think I found them? Amongst poor Cousin Lilly's things, of all places.' Through her unflagging efforts, the Royal collection has been brought together . . .

For this reason the recovery of the matched emeralds owned by her grandmother, the Duchess of Cambridge, was an integral part of her commitment.

All members of the royal family have an understanding of heritage to a greater or lesser degree. The Duke of York's acceptance of the burden of kingship and Princess Margaret's spurning of her divorced suitor, Group Captain Peter Townsend, show that the Windsors have an acute awareness of their dynastic history and their personal obligation to a wider duty.

An understanding of the Windsor's unique position in the history of the nation and Commonwealth helps explain the bitterness and sense of betrayal that surrounded the Abdication of King Edward VIII. Not only had he deserted his country but he had also forsaken the values of his family, frittering away all the years of sacrifice and self-denial in one selfish gesture.

As Prince of Wales his feckless, extravagant behaviour seemed to bring together the two dissolute strains in the Windsor and Teck families, previously exemplified by Prince Frank of Teck and King Edward VII. His spending on clothes echoed the days of the Prince Regent and provoked the disapproval of the King who had no time for his eldest son's sharp suits and raffish style. As a result he always had two pairs of trousers made – one with the creases down the front which the King considered spivvish, the other with creases down the sides in the approved naval fashion. Often royal distaste flared into open insult. When the Prince was well into his thirties, his father was heard to bellow at him, 'You dress like a cad. You act like a cad. You are a cad. Get out!'

This rumbustious relationship did not curb his spending, and with an income of around £100,000 ($442,000) a year from the Duchy of Cornwall estates he could well afford it. He bought and refurbished the baroque mansion of Fort Belvedere – then the most significant royal land purchase since Sandringham – but still retained a considerable income to fund his love of fashion. A glance through his order cards at his London outfitters, Hawes and Curtis, tells the story of his dandyism. Hardly a day would pass but that the Prince of Wales would stroll in and order '26 zephyr shirts, 12 soft collars, 12 stiff collars, 4 taffeta shirts, one tie' (13th December 1922) and then two days later '6 shirts' and the following day '1 yellow Shetland sweater' and so on, year after year. As one visitor to his apartments at St James's Palace remarked drily, 'There is no truth to the

OPPOSITE: *Imperious Queen Mary in her Coronation robes. The stunning diamond collet necklace has been worn by five generations of the royal family.*

Fort Belvedere in Berkshire. It was here that Wallis Simpson held court and where the details of the king's abdication were decided by the royal family and their advisors.

rumour that the Prince has 2,000 suits. When one considers how much time he spends choosing one suit, he wouldn't have time to choose 2,000.'

He was just as lavish with his spending on gifts for his various mistresses. He gave expensive jewels to Mrs Dudley Ward and Thelma, Lady Furness, and as early as 1925 newspaper cartoons showed him going into Cartier in Paris surrounded by a cluster of decorative women.

However, it was on the twice-divorced American, Wallis Simpson, for whom he reserved his greatest extravagance, a magnificent obsession that almost toppled the House of Windsor. As Society diarist Sir Henry 'Chips' Channon noted, 'Her collection of jewels is the talk of London ... Cartier's are resetting

magnificent, indeed fabulous jewels for Wallis and for what purpose if she is not to be Queen?' His generosity towards Mrs Simpson was boundless – 'literally smothered in jewels' said Channon admiringly after seeing her at a Society dinner party.

The suspicion grew that such lavishness could only be sustained if the Prince was giving away the royal family's heritage. It was widely rumoured that he had given the divorcee from Baltimore emeralds bequeathed to him by Queen Alexandra. While the Queen had made no will – and ordered her private papers to be burnt after her death – it was known that she had stated that she wanted the Prince of Wales to have some jewels 'for his wife', naturally believing that she would be the future Queen.

Gossip grew that the Prince was 'stealing' the family's birthright, fuelling wild and outlandish rumours about Mrs Simpson's jewellery. During the Abdication crisis it was suggested that her solicitor, Theodore Goddard, flew to France with the express intention of trying to claw back the Alexandra emeralds. The reality was rather different. Edward VIII himself ordered Goddard to Cannes when he discovered to his horror that the President of the Family Division had ordered the King's Proctor to investigate her divorce suit. However, the story refused to die. A decade later in 1946 when her jewel case was stolen it was suggested that the royal family had organized the robbery to regain the missing royal pieces.

The truth is more prosaic. The emeralds were purchased from Cartier in Paris, a fact surely known to Queen Mary who, while not approving of a woman she called an 'adventuress', did not stir herself over Mrs Simpson's finery in the way she did over the Cambridge emeralds. Her only comment, made to her lady-in-waiting, Lady Airlie, was the mild observation, 'He gives Mrs Simpson the most beautiful jewels.'

Queen Mary and the rest of the royal family were tenacious when it came to preserving their heritage during the ebb and flow of the Abdication crisis in late 1936. The discussions between the King, his brother, the Duke of York, the Prime Minister, Stanley Baldwin, and various private secretaries and lawyers ranged from amicable club talk to the increasingly bitter and rancorous exchanges of letters. During the course of the protacted wranglings over the Duke of Windsor's entitlements several principles were established regarding private and Crown property, precedents which appear partial and predisposed towards the established order.

A measure of the personal hostility Edward faced from those deciding his future is shown in the exchange that took place during the 1920s between Sir Alan Lascelles, his former private secretary, and Stanley Baldwin. In 1927 he told the future Prime Minister that 'the Prince of Wales would never be fit to reign and that the best thing that could happen was that he should break his neck in a point to point race.' Baldwin nodded in agreement. 'God forgive me, I have often thought the same,' he demurred.

King Edward was particularly incensed over the way his plans to sell his father's stamp collection were blocked. While he had never been interested in George V's abiding passion, he realized that these 365 rich red-leather volumes would secure his financial future. As arguments raged round the rooms of his

Sir William Orpen's portrait of the future Edward VIII at St Andrew's golf club.

country home at Fort Belvedere, only to be continued in offices at Buckingham Palace, King Edward was grudgingly forced to concede that as most of the stamps had been given to the King by subjects and Governments from all over the Commonwealth, then the collection belonged to the nation. In his last days in England, Edward became increasingly frustrated at the behaviour of the new King's men. One account claimed, 'At one point he became so angry at what he felt was their unfair treatment of him that he flew into a rage and hurled account books and ledgers onto the floor.'

Mrs Simpson, under seige in France, telephoned Fort Belvedere daily urging the King to stick to his guns. His financial adviser Sir Edward Peacock, a former Governor of the Bank of England, was present in the Fort during the interminable quarrelling over money. He noted 'the insistence over the telephone of the lady that he should fight for his rights. She kept up that line until near the end, maintaining that he was King and that his popularity would carry everything . . .'

Edward VIII was certainly right to be angry about the way he was prevented from taking at

The Duchess of Windsor's diamond ring and sapphire and diamond bracelet, inscribed 'For our contract 18–V–37', given to her by the Duke of Windsor before her marriage.

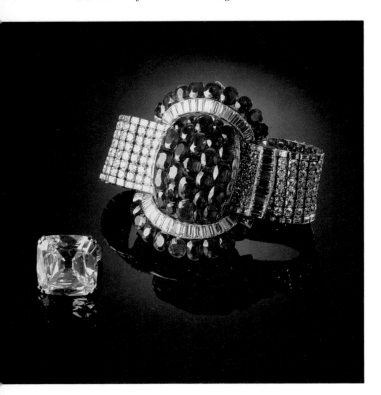

least part of the stamp collection into exile. While the majority of stamps were donated, a substantial proportion were bought privately, particularly in the years preceding the First World War. The legal historian Michael Nash observes, 'Reading through accounts of those last days one can almost feel the distaste many felt towards a king who had denied his birthright. Undoubtedly this coloured a number of rulings regarding what was considered Crown and personal property. Ownership of the stamp collection was not as clear cut as authority would have us believe.'

Nevertheless, that decision set a precedent, mentioned by the Lord Chamberlain, Lord Cobbold, during the Parliamentary hearings on the Civil List in 1971:

The Stamp Collections made by Kings George V and VI, though they are private collections, are, for practical purposes, regarded and operated in a similar way to the Royal Collection of Pictures and Works of Art. In no practical sense does the Queen regard any of these items as being at her free personal disposal.

In his will George V had left the private estates of Sandringham and Balmoral to his eldest son together with the royal heirlooms which naturally included his stamp collection. However, like Queen Victoria, the late King had left his eldest son out of the reckoning when it came to distributing his personal fortune. The bulk was settled on Queen Mary with adequate rather than generous allowances for his children.

George V still lived in the Victorian age in terms of finance and felt his children should do the same. In 1929 when Sir Edward Peacock took over from Lord Revelstoke as the Receiver-General of the Duchy of Cornwall he soon discovered the King's understanding of 'extravagance'. Peacock, the son of a Canadian congregationalist Minister, was the senior partner at Baring Brothers, the merchant bank who have traditionally directed the fortunes of the Duchy. He was approached by the Duke of York who found himself facing financial problems because of a large insurance policy he had taken out on the Duchess's life. Peacock reviewed his accounts, discovered that while there was no unnecessary expenditure, the insurance policy of £1,800 ($9,748) was causing problems. He suggested that the King should be asked to pay the sum yearly, deducting it from the legacy allocated to his second son in his will. However, neither the Duke nor his courtiers dared suggest this to the King. So Peacock reluctantly agreed to approach him. When he presented the case the King almost started from his chair saying, 'Nonsense, these children of mine are extravagant, they get much more than I did at that age and I made do.'

Peacock stood his ground and replied, 'Times have changed and I believe there is no extravagance. Furthermore this is money to be put away because he wanted to assure his wife's security.'

The King continued to quibble, repeating, 'No, no, positively no,' which effectively terminated the interview. When the King died Peacock learned with some professional satisfaction that the King had followed his advice exactly and had granted the Duke of York an advance on his legacy.

However, the King's strict attitude over money matters did engender problems for his younger sons which Peacock endeavoured to solve. In the 1930s Prince Henry, Duke of Gloucester, bought Barnwell Manor in Northamptonshire, spending £34,000 ($164,560) on the 5,000-acre estate – the bulk of his royal legacy. Overspending on machinery and new buildings soon brought him financial worries. He asked Peacock to spend the weekend at the farm to analyse the business. He went through the accounts and advised how, under a balanced scheme of improvements, the debt could be wiped out. His plan was duly adopted and the Duke's estate soon moved into profit. However, the Duke ungratefully refused to pay Peacock's brokerage commission arguing that his weekend visit to his farm was pleasure not business.

While Sir Edward was happy to advise the King's younger sons – with or without thanks – his main task was supervising the Duchy of Cornwall estates which he undertook with complete integrity. Lord Monckton, the Duke of Windsor's adviser, recalled:

Since this was royal property it was up to those in charge to set a high standard, the royal prince had to play the part of a model landlord and on matters sometimes far removed from account books and investments, Peacock remained the eminently sensible, far-seeing adviser. He looked at it in terms of the national interest and the prestige of the royal house.

The Duchess' flamingo brooch sold for £497,942 ($846,501) in 1987 – seven times the valuation.

During the Abdication crisis it was Peacock who played a central role, steadying the nerves of the usually unruffled Prime Minister, Stanley Baldwin, and his royal clients, Edward VIII and the Duke of York, while attempting to secure a satisfactory financial solution to a crisis without precedent.

His own memories of those days of strain and high drama, preserved by his friend Professor Graham, differ markedly from the impression conveyed by the Duke of Windsor's historian, Michael Bloch. He describes Peacock as 'critical of the king and hostile to Mrs Simpson' and says his influence with the Duke waned as a result.

Since 1929, when he had taken over financial control of the Duchy of Cornwall, Peacock had built up a friendly relationship with the Prince of Wales who was much more interested and knowledgeable about finance than his father.

INSTRUMENT OF ABDICATION

I, Edward the Eighth, of Great Britain, Ireland, and the British Dominions beyond the Seas, King, Emperor of India, do hereby declare My irrevocable determination to renounce the Throne for Myself and for My descendants, and My desire that effect should be given to this Instrument of Abdication immediately.

In token whereof I have hereunto set My hand this tenth day of December, nineteen hundred and thirty six, in the presence of the witnesses whose signatures are subscribed.

SIGNED AT
FORT BELVEDERE
IN THE PRESENCE
OF

Edward VIII's Instrument of Abdication witnessed by his brothers. Gentlemanly discussions about money soon degenerated into acid exchanges.

He liked to talk about investments and markets regardless of his private intentions. 'He showed a shrewd understanding of such matters,' recalled Peacock, whose advice helped the Prince amass a personal fortune of £1 million ($4.86 million) from his estates. When he abdicated, the Duke held £800,000 ($3,888,000) in investments, in spite of the large sums spent refurbishing Fort Belvedere and running a loss-making ranch in Alberta in Canada, together with the jewellery lavished on Mrs Simpson. As George V's younger sons, the Duke of York, the Duke of Gloucester and the Duke of Kent, had inherited around £50,000 ($243,000) each, there was a vast discrepancy

in personal wealth, a factor which may well have contributed to the hostility shown towards Edward VIII.

During the Abdication crisis Peacock was present at Fort Belvedere for all the crucial meetings to discuss the transfer of the family fortune from Edward VIII to the Duke of York. Lord Monckton recalled in 1959:

Even Baldwin leaned heavily on Peacock. The negotiations were very delicate, involving many adjustments. For example, George V had not allowed for the Duke of York's accession and had thought he was sufficiently cared for. How should the estates be divided, who should get Balmoral and Sandringham? Peacock stepped in, got to the heart of the matter, satisfied the Duke and Edward VIII on essential matters and then turned it over to the lawyers for legal drafting and precision.

He managed courtiers and politicians alike with consummate skill. Monckton was deeply impressed by the impeturbability of a basically shy man:

Peacock was a sentimental soul, was fond of Edward and deeply distressed. He cared greatly yet remained on the surface unruffled – a remarkable factor in his success in delicate negotiations.

Peacock recalled that he was able to buck up the Duke of York who he described as 'fearful and shaken – devoted to his brother to whom he looked up'. As the day approached for the fateful transfer of authority, the Duke became increasingly on edge as he faced what Queen Elizabeth was to call the 'intolerable honour' of kingship.

On 10th December 1936, after Edward VIII had signed the Instrument of Abdication, he met the Duke for what George VI subsequently described as 'a terrible lawyer interview which terminated quietly and harmoniously'. They finally reached an agreement over the private royal estates of Balmoral and Sandringham together with the heirlooms bequeathed to the Prince of Wales in George V's will. In return for handing them to his younger brother, Edward VIII would receive an annual income of £25,000 ($121,500) from the Duchy of Lancaster, subject to certain conditions, one of

OPPOSITE: *Following his marriage to Wallis Simpson, friends noted that the Duke of Windsor's generous nature rapidly altered. He became obsessed by the Stock Market and was adept at avoiding meal bills.*

which was that he would not see Mrs Simpson until after the Civil List became law.

The brothers had hoped that the Prime Minister and Chancellor of Exchequer, Neville Chamberlain, would be able to convince Parliament to grant the agreed sum to the new Duke of Windsor, though Baldwin had warned that this promise was conditional on the Opposition agreeing to this proposal. The Opposition opposed it and the Duke, by then living in effective exile in an Austrian mansion

OPPOSITE: The Duchess of Windsor's fabulous menagerie of diamonds included Cartier's tiger and panther bracelets. BELOW: A zoo of splendidly savage beasts bought by the adoring Duke. He purchased several with insurance money from the Sunningdale robbery.

owned by the Rothschilds, now started an acrimonious correspondence with his brother and advisers when it became apparent that the carefully judged agreement was now void.

He first threatened to keep Sandringham and Balmoral and then, following a meeting with Monckton, sent a letter to the King where he argued that the annual payment should not be related to his private means. The Duke, who had taken £800,000 ($3,888,000) with him — twice the Civil List payment granted to the new King — wrote plaintively, 'While naturally not mentioning what I have been able to save as Prince of Wales, I did tell you that I was very badly off, which indeed I am considering the position I shall have to maintain and what I have given up.' A few weeks later, during that

ABOVE: *Queen Mary's parting gift to her eldest son, the Duke of Windsor, as he began his long exile.*
OPPOSITE: *This pearl necklace and earrings were worn by the Duchess of Windsor at her husband's funeral in England in 1972 to general surprise.*

was ill prepared and a royal family who saw the modern-day equivalent of £25 million ($1,215,000) slipping from its grasp, the slights and injustice felt by the Duke of Windsor could be viewed as the whining of a man who had cut and run. Finally, in February 1938 – several months after the Duke and Duchess had visited Nazi Germany – a settlement was reached.

The Duke received a little over £10,000 ($48,600) from the interest on his notional sale of the royal estates and this income together with a further voluntary contribution of £10,000 ($48,600) a year from the King brought his annual income to the revised amount of £21,000 ($102,060). When the King died, the Duke managed to convince the present Queen to maintain the voluntary payment of £10,855 ($30,394) – but only after a long battle with the hostile Court. The House of Windsor was saved – but at a high price.

Abdication changed everything – not least the Duke's attitude towards money. During his days as Prince of Wales he was generous to a fault, regularly tipping doormen £5 ($24) and happily writing cheques for financially embarrassed friends. When he left Britain he became obsessively parsimonious, religiously reading the Stock Market reports and striking a balance for his books at the end of every trading day. After he married Mrs Simpson it was as if he had crossed a frontier into an alien country and become a different person, a penny pincher who wouldn't spend sixpence unless it was wrenched out of him.

Naturally the Duchess was the exception to this rule, spending millions of pounds on jewels and gowns, while the Duke treated his loyal advisers extremely shabbily. Lord Monckton, who served him devotedly for thirty years, received a pair of gold cufflinks for his efforts. As a final insult his name was spelt incorrectly in the engraving.

The Duke became notorious for enjoying a good meal and leaving the bill to others – as his biographer Charles Murphy discovered to his cost. He and his wife were invited to dine with the Duke and Duchess at the luxury Berkeley Hotel in Paris. The Duke ordered caviar, smoked salmon and vodka before the Duchess delivered the *coup de grâce*. 'Charlie, hadn't you better pick the wine?' she asked. Murphy recalls, 'I knew the knife blade had gone in to my back. It was a work of art in skipping the cheque.'

brooding, bitter summer of 1937 the Duke continued to lavish gifts on his future bride, spending £6,320 ($30,715) with Van Cleef and Arpels and £1,000 ($4,860) with Cartier, both Parisian jewellers.

In various letters he accused Buckingham Palace of 'behaving abominably', dismissed alternative proposals as 'unfair and intolerable' and described the labyrinthine negotiations as 'unpleasant'. At one point the King refused to accept further telephone calls about this vexed matter from his slighted elder brother.

In a world teetering on the brink of the cataclysm of war, with a stuttering, shy King attempting to grapple with a role for which he

In Britain the storm clouds of war were gathering and for the new King and Queen it was hardly a time to think of expanding the Windsor heritage, simply of surviving. The great works of art were carefully packaged and sent in Army trucks to caves in the Welsh hills while the stamp collection, which the Duke of Windsor had so coveted, was removed from its steel-lined room in Buckingham Palace. Queen Elizabeth learned how to handle small arms, the Princesses were sent to Windsor Castle while the King stayed among his people in London. Typically the Queen turned down Chamberlain's offer to sail to Canada and safety. 'The children won't leave without me, I won't leave without the King and the King will never leave,' she said stoutly. They endured the same strict rationing as the rest of the country – albeit eating their macaroni or egg flip off exquisite china – and felt a further kinship with the nation when Buckingham Palace itself suffered bomb damage. 'Now I can look the East End in the face,' was the Queen's famous remark.

In 1942 the Queen sensibly commissioned the artist John Piper to paint a series of twenty-eight watercolours of Windsor Castle in case that too was bombed. Her artistic sensibility – she is now a knowledgeable collector of porcelain and Impressionist paintings – was clearly not shared by the King. He was shown the completed set of paintings after morning service at St George's Chapel one Sunday. After gazing silently at each picture of delicately tinted stone against a brooding, forbidding sky he remarked, 'You have been unfortunate with the weather, haven't you, Mr Piper.'

After the war the wealthy invested in art – the price of Old Masters soared dramatically – but the King patriotically gave instructions that his private wealth should be invested in British industries and so help with the work of reconstruction.

He was also concerned to help his German relatives who had fallen on hard times in that bleak, divided nation. For a time the world's most expensive book, entitled the *Gospels of Henry Lion*, which sold for £7.4 million ($17.2 million) in 1983, came into royal hands. Ironically it was loaned to the King by the Prince of Hanover – the same kingdom involved in endless litigation with Queen Victoria – as financial security.

Perhaps the brightest spot in this austere fifteen-year reign was the marriage of Princess Elizabeth to Prince Philip. Even this royal occasion did not escape the draconian effects of rationing. There was concern in the Cabinet of the Labour Government that the silk for the dress should not be imported and then, when it was confirmed that the silk was from Britain, that the silkworms themselves were not Japanese or Italian.

The royal designer, Normal Hartnell, recalled, 'Was I so guilty of treason that I would deliberately use enemy silk worms?' He contacted his Scottish silk supplier to ascertain the nationality of the worms. 'Our worms,' came the proud reply, 'are Chinese worms – from Nationalist China, of course.'

Tactfully the King limited his Civil List request for the young couple. He told Parliament that he was anxious 'not to impose a burden on his people at a time when they are faced with grave economic difficulties' and agreed to shoulder £100,000 ($280,000) of the increase from the savings of running a limited Court during the war.

However, the wedding gifts to the future Queen and her Consort revealed a world beyond the penny-pinching style to which the nation had become accustomed. The Nizam of Hyderabad presented a diamond bandeau tiara and matching necklace, King Farouk an ancient Egyptian necklace, while the jewels from the King and Queen and Queen Mary, which included a diamond festoon and scroll tiara and Indian ruby and diamond necklace, gave an indication of the sunshine of opulence lurking above the grey skies of austerity Britain.

Nonetheless, Queen Mary was careful to warn her family about her Hungarian relations who were 'crawling out of the woodwork' during the wedding celebrations. 'They should be ignored at all costs,' she cautioned, mindful that the Windsor heritage should not be dissipated. She was most careful about her own will, changing it three times as potential benefactors predeceased her. When she died in 1953 she left her fabulous collection of jewellery amassed during a lifetime of obsessive acquisition to the Queen, who had also inherited the family property and heirlooms in the trust of

OPPOSITE: *George VI's image of a quietly devoted family man vividly contrasted with the lavish life style of his brother, the Duke of Windsor.*

her father, George VI, who had died one year before his mother in 1952. As with previous monarchs, the late King left the bulk of his private estate to his widow and Princess Margaret, enabling Queen Elizabeth the Queen Mother, to purchase the remote and ramshackle Castle of Mey on the bleak, blustery north coast of Scotland.

The present reign, immediately christened the New Elizabethan Age, marked a resurgence in royal fortunes, heralded by the launching of the royal yacht *Britannia* – the only example of innovative royal building seen in this reign apart from the new home of the Duke and Duchess of York.

While austerity lingered on – during *Britannia's* maiden voyage sheets from the days of Queen Victoria were brought into service – Prince Philip brought the dynamism and verve evident during his naval career to bear on the House of Windsor. His energy was much needed. Since the accession of George V in 1910, virtually nothing had been done to revitalize or modernize the royal estates. Even

Following the death of her husband, George VI, the Queen Mother spent years restoring her Scottish retreat, the Castle of Mey, to its former glory.

Edward VIII during his brief reign grasped the immensity of the task in hand. Of Sandringham he noted, 'There in remote Norfolk by the Wash, my father's private war with the twentieth century had ended in almost complete repulse of the latter.' He described the property as a 'voracious white elephant' and deputed his brother, the future George VI, and a mutual friend, Lord Radnor, to prepare a report on the estate. However, as Prince Philip was to discover, the King found that he was a 'prisoner of the past' and that any 'tampering with tradition' was fraught with difficulties.

Prince Philip is made of sterner stuff. 'He is a hard man but thank goodness the royal family had someone like him,' admitted a member of the Household. 'He put the whole shooting match on a much more busineslike footing.' He has done much to bring the royal family into the late twentieth century without compromising its essential nature. Buckingham Palace is now computerized, with everything from stock control to standard letters on disc, and yet this has not affected the mystique of monarchy.

In a similar way he focused his energy on Balmoral and Sandringham and made them more professional and cost-effective. The Norfolk estate now runs at a profit, providing

blackcurrants for a well-known brand of cordial, peas and beans for the freezer factory at King's Lynn and pick-your-own apples for autumn visitors. In the 1960s the Queen decided to demolish ninety-one rooms at the main house while modernizing the rest.

As the Prince explained in the preface to Ralph Whitlock's book, *Royal Farmers*, 'When I first went to Sandringham over thirty years ago, some of the tenanted farms were still being worked by horses. Gangs of female labour were contracted to lift the vegetable crops . . . a pattern not much changed in 200 years.' At Balmoral the Prince initiated a forestry pro-gramme, while on Prince Albert's model farm at Windsor reforms were introduced which meant that the royal palaces were supplied with milk, cheese and eggs from the royal dairies.

The same cost-conscious approach was adopted towards the royal family's public role when Prince Philip invited the industrialist Sir Basil Smallpiece into the red-carpeted corri-dors of Buckingham Palace to supervise an efficiency drive. Prince Philip was horrified to discover, for example, that when he wanted a

The 5,700-ton royal yacht Britannia, *built in 1952, is the Queen's floating palace.*

plate of sandwiches it took four men to convey the royal command to the kitchens.

In 1969 it was his off-the-cuff remarks in America about the royal family going 'into the red' which, for the first time since Queen Victoria, led to a Parliamentary Committee inquiry into the Civil List. While he made flippant remarks about selling his polo ponies and moving into a smaller house his statement took on greater significance given the fact that during the reign, various Government departments had taken on expenditure tradi-tionally covered by the Civil List. Thus in 1952 the Ministry of Defence shouldered the run-ning costs of the royal yacht *Britannia* and the Queen's Flight, while in 1972 the Government Hospitality Fund took over the remaining expense of State visits to Britain – 130 years after Queen Victoria first complained of the imposition.

Normally the Civil List (the payment to the sovereign to maintain the Royal Household and cover costs incurred in fulfilling duties as Head of State), is settled within six months of the start of a reign and remains constant there-after. As a result of the Prince's outspoken remarks much heat but very little light was generated by the Parliamentary review of royal

81

finances. In spite of the presence of senior MPs, including the former Prime Minister, Harold Wilson, and previous Chancellors of the Exchequer, very little headway was made in trying to ascertain the Queen's private fortune. In a masterly report by her Lord Chamberlain, Lord Cobbold, a former Governor of the Bank of England, the Committee's minds were guided firmly to the expenditure incurred on behalf of the monarch's public duties. In a prepared statement he told MPs:

The Queen has her own private funds . . . Her Majesty handles these matters herself, as did the late King and earlier Sovereigns.

In view of the publicity on this particular matter, the Queen has instructed me to make certain comments to the Committee on her behalf. Her Majesty has been much concerned by the astronomical figures which have been bandied about in some quarters suggesting that the value of these funds may now run into fifty to a hundred million pounds ($90–240 million) or more . . . She wishes me to assure the Committee that these suggestions are wildly exaggerated.

Britannia's comfortable drawing-room. Prince Albert designed the gimbal table.

While republican MP William Hamilton railed at the Queen's Gracious Message of 19th May, 1971 as the 'most insensitive and brazen pay claim made in the last 200 years', Parliament accepted the recommendations for a doubling of the Civil List. Three years later in 1975 the depredations of inflation required a further adjustment. Since then the Civil List has been raised annually in line with inflation.

From the time of that Parliamentary inquiry, a number of estimates of the Queen's funds invested in stocks and shares have been made. For example, the American financial magazine *Fortune* calculated that in 1987 her investment portfolio was worth just £1.9 billion ($3.3 billion), giving the Queen an annual income from her shares of around £18 million ($30.6 million). Other estimates, while differing wildly, have all erred on the generous side. However, this presupposes that Lord Cobbold's original statement, authorized by the Queen, was false — which is inconceivable — or that royal investments have hugely outperformed the norm for the Stock Market.

A more realistic up-to-date estimate, based on the performance of the top 700 companies in the Stock Market since 1971, would put the Queen's private shareholding in 1989 at

A rare picture of Princesses Elizabeth and Margaret handling money, in the form of Savings Bonds, during a visit to the Post Office.

between £350 and £400 million ($595–$680 million) in both capital and tax-free dividend income. Not bad for someone who as a child received the princely sum of five pence a week pocket money and at the tender age of thirteen showed her thrifty nature by managing to amass the king's ransom of £30 ($115) in her Savings Bank account held at the Kensington Headquarters of the Post Office.

During the 1970s and early 1980s the Queen embarked on a programme of quiet consolida-tion where she invested around £4.5 million ($10.44 million) on land for herself – enlarging the Balmoral estate and purchasing the stables at West Ilsley, Berkshire – and for her children in the form of wedding presents. In 1976 she paid £720,000 ($1,728,000) for Gatcombe Park for Princess Anne and is also paying the building costs – estimated at £1 million ($1.7 million) – for the Duke and Duchess of York's home at Sunninghill. Indeed, it is a sign of the Queen's private prosperity that this conven-tional, conservative monarch has felt able to break with royal tradition and give her children both family jewellery and property for their wedding gifts.

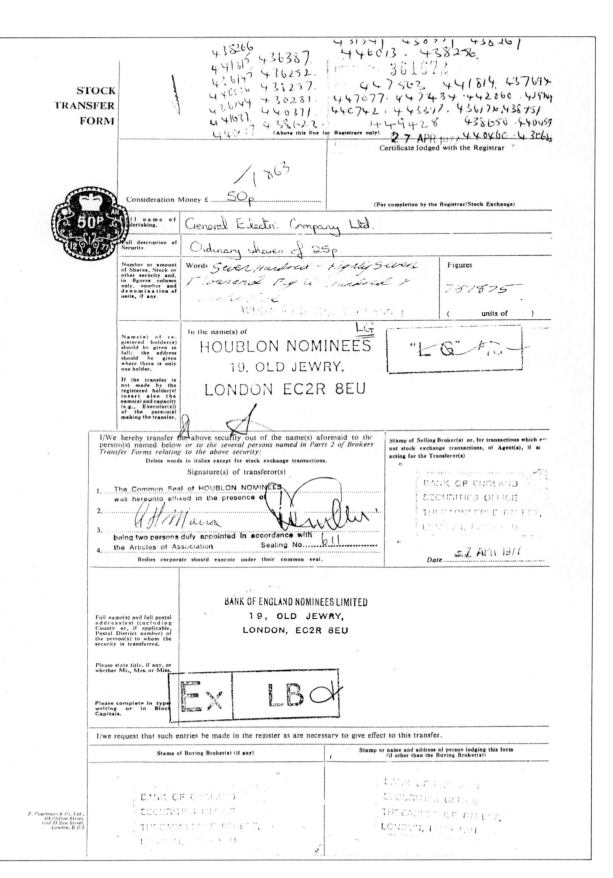

STOCK
TRANSFER
FORM

438266 436387.
44131 436252.
42617 431257.
440044 430281.
436244 440371.
441637 438622.

431241 430371 438261
446013. 438256.
361872
447563 441814 437694
447077 447434 442060 437441
440742. 443347. 436178.438751
449428 438650.440459
440060 436437

(Above this line for Registrars only)

27 APR 1977

Certificate lodged with the Registrar

Consideration Money £ ......50p.

(For completion by the Registrar/Stock Exchange)

50P
12 4 77

Full name of Undertaking.   General Electric Company Ltd.

Full description of Security.   Ordinary shares of 25p

Number or amount of Shares, Stock or other security and, in figures column only, number and denomination of units, if any.

Words Seven hundred eighty seven Thousand eight hundred & seventy five

Figures 787875

(units of)

Name(s) of registered holders(s) should be given in full; the address should be given where there is only one holder.

If the transfer is not made by the registered holder(s) insert also the name(s) and capacity (e.g., Executor(s) of the person(s) making the transfer.

In the name(s) of

HOUBLON NOMINEES
19, OLD JEWRY,
LONDON EC2R 8EU

LG
"LG" F0

I/We hereby transfer the above security out of the name(s) aforesaid to the person(s) named below or to the several persons named in Parts 2 of Brokers Transfer Forms relating to the above security:

Delete words in italics except for stock exchange transactions.

Signature(s) of transferor(s)

1. The Common Seal of HOUBLON NOMINEES was hereunto affixed in the presence of

2. A.H. Mann

3. being two persons duly appointed in accordance with the Articles of Association   Sealing No.......611

4.

Bodies corporate should execute under their common seal.

Stamp of Selling Broker(s) or, for transactions which are not stock exchange transactions, of Agent(s), if any acting for the Transferor(s)

BANK OF ENGLAND
SECURITIES OFFICE
THE CADWELL STREET,
LONDON, EC2R 8EU

27 APR 1977

Date

Full name(s) and full postal address(es) (including County or, if applicable, Postal District number) of the person(s) to whom the security is transferred.

BANK OF ENGLAND NOMINEES LIMITED
19, OLD JEWRY,
LONDON, EC2R 8EU

Please state title, if any, or whether Mr., Mrs. or Miss.

Please complete in typewriting or in Block Capitals.

Ex   LBd

I/we request that such entries be made in the register as are necessary to give effect to this transfer.

Stamp of Buying Broker(s) (if any)

BANK OF ENGLAND
SECURITIES OFFICE
THE CADWELL STREET,
LONDON EC2R 8EU

Stamp or name and address of person lodging this form (if other than the Buying Broker(s))

BANK OF ENGLAND
SECURITIES OFFICE
THE CADWELL STREET,
LONDON, EC2R 8EU

F. Couchman & Co. Ltd.,
418 Clifton Street,
and 33 Sun Street,
London, E.C.2

84

OPPOSITE: *The secrecy of the Queen's shares are protected by a Bank of England Nominee account. In 1977 it is thought her shares in GEC and RTZ were transferred there from the Houblon account.*

Lord Snowdon received a cash sum from Princess Margaret as a divorce settlement.

Another sign of the affluence of the dynasty came in the unlikely form of the divorce settlement agreed between Princess Margaret and Lord Snowdon. Normally the husband is legally bound to financially provide for his former spouse. However, in 1978 Princess Margaret, a millionairess in her own right, settled a substantial sum, estimated at a little over £100,000 ($230,000) to enable Lord Snowdon to buy a house in Kensington.

Doubtless alarmed by the comment aroused by the Parliamentary Select Committee, the Queen acted in the 1970s to further remove discussion of her private fortune from the public domain. In the wake of numerous City scandals, which the then Prime Minister, Edward Heath, called 'the unacceptable face of capitalism', the Government planned to introduce a Companies Act to help regulate the Stock Market by the compulsory disclosure of share ownership. However, while the Bill was being drawn up the telephone lines between Buckingham Palace and Downing Street were busy as the Queen's then Private Secretary Sir Martin Charteris, now Lord Charteris and Provost of Eton, discussed the implications with his opposite number, Mr Robert (now Lord) Armstrong. Under the terms of the Bill the Queen's private shareholdings would be open to public scrutiny. The problem exercised the minds of officials in several Government departments, including Trade and Industry, as a suitable solution was sought.

In a letter dated 5th December, 1973, Mr Armstrong wrote to a Department of Trade official, Mr Hird, stating:

The Prime Minister has seen your letter. He has asked me to say that he will attach great importance to arrangements which protect the Queen's private shareholdings from disclosure. Since this has been raised with me (though not with the Prime Minister) by the Palace I should be grateful to be kept informed of developments.

The issue was resolved by forming a new shareholding company, Bank of England Nominees Ltd, which was specifically exempt from the provisions of the proposed Companies Act. However, this company would only hold securities on behalf of Heads of State and their immediate family, or bodies closely allied to Governments. It was agreed that holdings over five per cent in a company would result in the identity of the owner being disclosed.

Lord Limerick, the then Secretary of State at the Department of Trade and Industry, congratulated all concerned on a 'neat and defensible solution to the problem of the nominee holdings provisions for the Queen's private shareholdings'. The Queen's solicitors, William Farrer and Company, commented that it was a 'perfectly reasonable' resolution of the issue.

The Bill did not become law until 1976. The intervening three years saw a row over the leaking of confidential memos on the matter to the Communist daily newspaper, the *Morning Star*, and a change of Government, from Conservative to Labour. However, the new administration adopted the same exclusion clause to protect the Queen and other Heads of State from inquiry.

The result of this legislation has been to cocoon further the royal finances in a web of mystery. Journalists who delve into dusty share registers find the impenetrable phrase 'Bank of England Nominees' staring back at them when they try to find a hint of royal involvement in a specific company.

The only reliable way is to return to the share registers of April 1977 – when the new Companies Act came into force – and examine the transfer of ownership from one nominee company to Bank of England Nominees. In that crucial month a survey of just thirty of the 3,000 quoted companies on the Stock Exchange revealed that Bank of England Nominees held £80 million ($186 million) worth of securities. Besides the royal family, the Sultan of Brunei – reputed to be the world's richest man – and numerous foreign Governments have taken advantage of the secrecy offered by Bank of England Nominees holdings.

So how to root out the Queen's shares? The only way is by cross checking with independent sources at the time the Act came into force. Private information from the Bank of England reveals that in 1977 the Queen held shares in the mining company, Rio Tinto Zinc (RTZ) and the electrical giant, GEC. An analysis of the 1977 share registeres of RTZ and GEC shows the transfer of shareholdings from two holding companies to Bank of England Nominees.

The shares were held by the Securities Management Trust AA Account and Houblon Nominees LG account. As the Securities Management Trust is held on behalf of Kuwait's Ministry of Finance, it may be concluded that the Houblon Nominees LG account is that administered for the Queen. In 1977 Houblon Nominees held 101,875 shares worth £244,500 ($567,240) in RTZ and at GEC the holding of 787,875 shares was worth £1,331,508 ($2,609,856). In 1977 the Queen's holdings in

those two companies alone amounted to over £1,576,000 ($3,656,320). Since the transfer to Bank of England Nominees the real owner of securities cannot be revealed.

Other members of the royal family are not quite so secretive. The 1987 accounts for the Duchy of Cornwall show that Prince Charles held £19,663,635 ($33,428,179) in stocks and shares – mainly equities. He has maintained the royal family's tradition of employing the senior partner at Baring Brothers, currently Sir John Baring, as the Duchy's Receiver-General.

The Princess of Wales, the Duke of York and Prince Edward all held modest holdings of 800 shares in British Telecom when it was privatized. The shares were held under Strand Nominees Limited, the designated accounts being: ANDG – Andrew Prince HRH; EDWK – Edward Prince HRH; R220 – Wales Her Royal Highness the Princess of.

While the day-to-day running of the Queen's portfolio is not her concern, she takes a well-informed interest in the City. Perhaps her curiosity was kindled as a youngster when she attended parties thrown by Lancelot Hugh Smith at his home Mount Clare, Roehampton in the 1930s. He employed the then Queen Elizabeth's favourite brother, Jock Bowes-Lyon, in the small but expanding stockbroking firm of Rowe and Pitman. It was at these parties that the families of the great and the good met – and a little discreet business was transacted. The stockbroking firm, founded in 1894, was once described as 'the best club in town', employing names from all the great banking families. It was no coincidence that Rowe and Pitman, together with James Capel, the oldest stockbrokers in the City, have handled the Queen's investments throughout her reign. Indeed, the Queen attended a private lunch at Capel's Old Broad Street offices in 1975 to celebrate the firm's bicentenary, an engagement not recorded in the Court Circular or elsewhere.

The register which shows that the Princess of Wales and Prince Edward held 800 shares in British Telecom following privatization.

Her concern about the new 'catch me if you can' morality in the deregulated City following Big Bang caused her to make an uncharacteristically forthright speech at the Guildhall in 1989. She warned, 'Rules and structures may be important but much more important are the unwritten rules and the will to abide by them. In the end it is the loyalty and good sense of the citizens themselves that makes the whole system work.'

Those words could serve as a fitting description of the evolution of the House of Windsor over the last 150 years. The dynasty has gained the trust of its people by its own good citizenship, sense of responsibility and dutiful housekeeping. It has stood by the values of honour and decency that its people have come to respect. They are one Family Firm – as George VI called them – where the bottom line is not the ultimate aim of their business.

For the most part the Windsors have firmly eschewed the obviously ostentatious, acutely aware of the impression they will make on their public by conspicuous display. 'Bad for the image,' remarked Prince Charles the day a Rolls-Royce replaced his ancient Aston Martin sports car as he prepared to drive to polo. When they are on official parade they use their limousines, helicopters, yachts and jewellery in the same way as an actor uses props on a stage.

Off duty they are careful to conceal their wealth while their private collections of paintings, *objets d'art* and furniture are neatly masked by their thoughtful stewardship of the Crown collections.

Edward VIII's unpopularity within the royal family was the result of his calculated high fashion, sparkling Society friends and glittering style which struck the wrong note during the austere 1930s.

It is a question of tone. Today the royal family shoot with Princes, hunt with Kings and mix with millionaires in much the same way as did Queen Victoria or King Edward VII. Yet their effortless hegemony has been secured because they still speak and act for Everyman.

Unlike their European counterparts, the House of Windsor has never mistaken Society for society.

Yet over the last 150 years their historic role as public figures has diminished while their private privileges have grown. The Windsors have shrewdly used the shield of their public duties to construct an armour of legal conces-

The Princess of Wales perches prettily on Prince Charles' ancient Aston Martin sports car.

sions, ranging from their wills to their shares, to deflect the arrows of outrageous inquiry.

It is a question of fine judgement for the royal family – and ultimately Parliament – about how long their legal and tax advantages, secured by dint of their public role, can coexist alongside their increasingly vocal demands to be left alone and treated as ordinary people. By the year 2001, barring accidents, the Queen's tax-free shareholdings alone will be worth £1 billion ($1.7 billion). When Prince Charles ascends the throne he will be the richest monarch in history and his son, Prince William, the wealthiest Prince of Wales. In a political climate that eschews traditional privileges, the royal family's wealth may come under intense scrutiny. The debate over the controversial community charge – which the Queen escapes by virtue of the Royal Prerogative – is a case in point.

Ironically the very success of the Windsor dynasty may prove to be its undoing.

3
In Glorious Tribute

The atmosphere at Bahrain airport was that of a light-hearted lynch party. Standing in one corner of the VIP lounge was the small but quietly defiant figure of Amit Roy, a *Sunday Times* reporter assigned to the tour of the Gulf States by the Prince and Princess of Wales in 1986. Facing him were the serried ranks of his accusers, journalists from the rest of Fleet Street outraged at a story he had written saying that the royal couple would be given jewellery worth more than £1 million ($1.7 million) by the oil-rich sheiks and sultans who were to be their hosts.

BELOW: *The Prince of Wales receiving an award from the Emir of Bahrain.*
OPPOSITE: *The Princess of Wales wears the superb sapphire and diamond necklace, crescent earrings and bracelet presented by the Sultan of Oman.*

What infuriated the media posse was that his account differed radically from the official Buckingham Palace line that the Prince and Princess would receive only token presents. On the strength of that statement one journalist representing the *News of the World* resigned in protest when the editor David Montgomery changed his front page for Roy's story when it appeared in the normally sober *Sunday Times*.

As tempers rose in the desert sun, Roy, a Bengali who came to study in Britain in 1961, kept his cool. He alluded to his sources within the Saudi Arabian court, saying softly that time would tell. As the media jet flew on to Riyadh in Saudi Arabia, the royal party's Press Secretary, the late Victor Chapman, made a point of announcing the official gifts from the Sultan of Oman. They comprised a dovecote and a painting. As this *coup de grâce* was delivered, a

journalist from one notorious tabloid paper leaned over to Roy and said in hurt tones, 'It's us who are supposed to make things up, Amit, not the *Sunday Times*.'

Almost exactly a year later the Princess appeared at a banquet in Bonn on her first official tour of West Germany. Looking radiant, the diamonds in her leaf and flower Spencer family tiara were complemented by sapphire and diamond crescent earrings, necklace and bracelet. The jewellery was modern, Middle Eastern – and worth millions of pounds. 'They were private gifts from the Sultan of Oman,' said a Palace official innocently. The secret was out. Several weeks later the Sultan's generosity was further revealed when Prince Charles took delivery of a brand new Aston Martin sports car costing around £80,000 ($136,000).

Roy's reputation was vindicated, and Buckingham Palace embarrassed. As one former member of the Wales' Household observed, 'Oh, the palaver we had over those damn jewels.' It explains why the privately proffered gifts from

BELOW: *During a visit to Dubai in 1979, Sheik Rashid presents the Queen with the gifts of a suite of diamond and sapphires and solid gold camel, now used as a table decoration on* Britannia.
OPPOSITE: *Camellia petals make a fragrant pathway for the Queen's progress in Oporto, Portugal.*

the Saudi Royal Family have not yet been seen in public. In fairness, the Palace's predicament was due as much to Arabian custom as to their own innate secrecy. They consider it 'vulgar' to discuss private gifts while discreetly attempting to outdo each other in the lavishness of their offerings to a Princess who they think is 'very special'.

This episode goes far beyond the immediate issue of how much the Prince and Princess of Wales were given during their tour of the Gulf. It raises the question about what is Crown and what is private royal property, and the wider issue of why give anything to a family who already have everything? In many ways tribute, the giving and receiving of tokens – however great or small – is the lifeblood of the royal family. For as members of the royal family they symbolize the values of national life, so tribute embodies traditional ideals of friendship and devotion to the nation and the royal House of Windsor. It echoes the feudal custom of swearing fealty to the lord by the act of giving, and even retains a quasi-religious significance.

The divinity of kings, the medieval belief which accorded the monarch special healing powers by virtue of his or her closeness to God, is still a powerful canon in the current idolatry towards the royal family. The Princess of Wales,

so often described as a fairytale Princess, has been endowed with these celestial qualities. When she visited the victims of the Manchester air disaster in 1985, her presence inspired one young woman to regain her sight in spite of her injuries. The saintliness ascribed to the Princess has been captured in a portrait showing her haloed in light, comforting a roomful of bedridden young men who were dying of the incurable AIDS virus.

The sacred nature of the royal family finds its fullest expression when the nation mourns the loss of one of its members. When Queen Mary died in 1953, the public queued night and day to shuffle past her coffin in Westminster Hall. Even the left-wing *Reynolds News* remarked on it:

For three days and nights they bowed, saluted, wept, crossed themselves and knelt to pray for the departed Queen. 'No religious service in recent years has ever evoked such a show of mass reverence,' said a priest. 'The church has certainly not canonised her. But the public sanctified her as no saint was publicly venerated at Westminster before.'

There is also the notion that the royal family must be lavishly rewarded as part of the unspoken agreement that they are surrendering their personal freedom for remorseless, selfless public duty. In the same way, Aztec slaves were given unlimited privileges before they were sacrificed to the Sun God. Thus liberty is exchanged for heaven on earth.

Queen Mary was both a pillar and architect of the modern House of Windsor. As Edward VIII recalled, 'To my mother the monarchy was something sacred and the Sovereign a personage apart.' She witnessed the highpoint of Imperial splendour under Queen Victoria and King Edward VII which was attended by the corresponding trappings of ceremonial. In the days when Cecil Rhodes remarked, 'To be born an Englishman is to draw a winning ticket in the lottery of life', Buckingham Palace was the perfect stage on which to celebrate the glory of an Empire without precedent. Within this world of effortless supremacy and assurance, the House of Windsor was at the summit of a deferential hierarchy, accepting tribute from the nations which made up its domain.

BELOW: *The Prince of Wales accepted lavish gifts, including a solid gold bed, from Indian Maharajahs during his tour in 1875.* OPPOSITE: *Queen Alexandra, festooned with the lavish fruits of Empire, wears the diamond crown ordered by Queen Victoria.*

ABOVE and OPPOSITE: *The Cambridge Lover's Knot tiara which Garrard made for Queen Mary in 1914, using pearls she had been given as a wedding present. The tiara was inherited by the Queen who gave it to the Princess of Wales as a wedding gift. She wears it here during a visit to Washington, 1985.*

The mines of the Transvaal and the vaults of the Indian royal families were the chief sources of tribute. For the assorted princes, nizams and maharajahs of India, a land where 'diamonds are as plentiful as blackberries in England', tribute was a symbol of deference as well as political self-interest. Under British rule, the Indian royal families maintained powerful sovereignty over their numerous kingdoms, an influence they lost after Partition in 1948.

In the days of Empire the royal family were proffered an embarrassment of riches. Pearls, diamonds, rubies and emeralds were the eager offerings of the Indian royal houses, anxious to outdo their rivals. Legend has it that in 1917 when *HMS Medina* – used as the official royal yacht for the Delhi Durbar six years earlier – returned home from the subcontinent she was laden with gifts for the royal family and other officials. The truth will never be known for she

was torpedoed by a German submarine off Start Point in Devon on the last leg of her journey. Tibetan jade and ivory *objets d'art* have been recovered from the wreck – but no jewellery as yet.

Since the Second World War, the sun has gone down on the Empire yet the glow of tribute continues to burnish the royal House. During the present reign the Windsors' reputation has expanded beyond that family of nations which now makes up the Commonwealth. They are the only international noble House and their lives are celebrated on a global scale. An estimated 1,000 million people watched the wedding of the Duke and Duchess of York on television – one of the largest audiences ever recorded. The Queen is also the most travelled monarch in history which has further fuelled the royal family's universal popularity.

When the Queen visited the Gulf States in 1979, the strongroom of the royal yacht *Britannia* was filled with lavish gifts from Arab sheiks who wished to show their affection and deference. Among the gifts were a silver dhow and double string of pearls from Kuwait, an 18-inch solid gold camel and palm tree hung with ruby dates from Sheikh Rashid of Dubai, lapis lazuli fruitstands with prancing gold horses encrusted with diamonds and a pearl and diamond necklace from the Emir of Qatar. For Prince Philip there were gold and platinum watches, together with a gold sword and a mother of pearl handle and a scabbard covered with rubies and diamonds. Customs officers were quoted as saying that the duty alone would have been £180,000 ($417,000) on these opulent offerings.

Since the days of Queen Victoria, the royal family have amassed, through tribute and acquisition, the greatest treasure trove in the world. 'We have too much already,' the Queen once said to the Marchioness of Cambridge when discussing reports that all the Duchess of Windsor's jewels should be given to the royal family.

While jewellery is the most expensive expression of esteem, tribute to the House of Windsor takes many forms. The hotelier who spent £50,000 ($85,000) on horses for Princess Anne to take part in a riding contest in Dubai, a £40,000 ($68,000) handwoven kimono for the Princess of Wales, a £2,500 ($4,250) camera for the Duke of York (which he promptly broke),

and a buffalo head for the Duke and Duchess of York are just some of the gifts the royal family have received over the last five years.

Each gift is catalogued and indexed, often to be brought out when a dignatory makes a return visit to Britain. Some, however, defy the usual procedures. Among the most bizarre gifts have been a crocodile in a biscuit tin, a giant tortoise, a live boa constrictor, a baby bear, a baby elephant complete with 100 avocado pears, three bunches of bananas and twenty tins of sugar, a forest by the waters of Galilee, a walkie talkie doll, 100 hot dogs with mustard, a bale of cotton and a nylon bikini.

Many of the thousands of mementoes and artefacts are deposited in the basement at Buckingham Palace or in the empty chapel at Kensington Palace where they join the countless other tiger's paws, Fijian canoes and ceremonial cloaks. The cash-conscious

LEFT, BELOW and OPPOSITE: *Gifts to the royal family come in a multitude of guises. The Duke and Duchess of York accepted a buffalo head during a visit to Canada in 1987 while a Dubai hotelier paid £50,000 ($85,000) for horses so that the Princess Royal could compete in a riding contest. After initial reluctance, the Princess of Wales wore a kimono for the cameras in Kyoto, Japan.*

LEFT: *The Windsor dynasty expressed in diamonds for Denis Fildes' portrait of the Queen Mother. She wore the George III fringe tiara – one of the few Hanoverian heirlooms – and diamond collet necklace, made for Queen Victoria.* RIGHT: *The Crown Prince and Princess of Jordan gave the Prince and Princess of Wales a stunning gold choker studded with gems.*

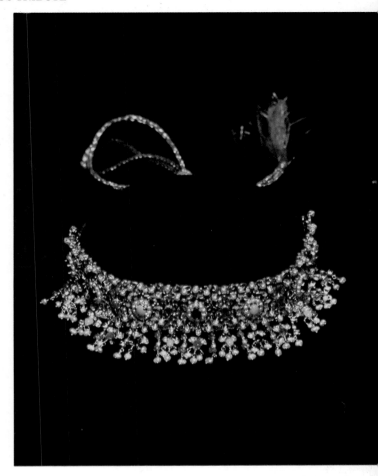

burghers of Newcastle-under-Lyme in Staffordshire were so concerned that their gift of a loving cup should not be ignored that they sought assurance from the Palace that the Queen would not neglect it. 'She looks at all her gifts two or three times a year,' soothed her Private Secretary.

These gifts underline the fact that the wealth of the Windsors is not only based on business, estates and happenstance, but primarily on the respect and adoration which is at the heart of the sacred trust endowed upon the majesty that is the House of Windsor.

Like the Church, the royal family receive frequent bequests from their subjects, perhaps hoping that it will smooth the path to their Maker. Under a Royal Charter of 1337 Prince Charles, as Duke of Cornwall, is entitled to the property of Duchy residents who die intestate. These monies – in 1983 alone he received £183,000 ($420,00) – go to charity as did the bequest of £10,000 ($23,000) an East End docker left to the Queen.

Most of the legacies the royal family receive are from friends and relatives. They leave the Windsors money, jewellery and artefacts especially where there is some royal significance. The millionairess Mrs Ronald Greville, who loaned her home of Polesden Lacey for the Duke and Duchess of York's honeymoon in 1923, left Queen Elizabeth her impressive pearl collection and a magnificent diamond ring, together with £20,000 ($76,600) to the teenage Princess Margaret. In the last decade the Queen and her family have been left historic letters and royal portraits for the Royal Collection, a Louis XIV clock, a set of naturalistic water colours estimated to be worth £200,000 ($464,000), a collection of Fabergé elephants, together with glass and silverware engraved with the royal monogram.

Care has always to be exercised to ensure that the royal family's name is not exploited or their position abused. Commercial firms who hope to reap the benefits of a royal connection have their wares politely but firmly refused, while people who are not known personally find their gifts, however generous, tactfully declined.

When Dr Armand Hammer first met Prince Charles at an exhibition of Winston Churchill's paintings in London his effusive generosity was diplomatically rebuffed. He recalls:

I had heard that, while his mother owned a Churchill painting, he had none. His enthusiasm for the pictures was so engaging that I offered him one I owned as a present. He demurred, saying that he could not accept it personally, so I offered it to the Queen's Jubilee Fund, and he very enthusiastically accepted.

On another occasion the Princess of Wales innocently accepted a gold and diamond ring, worth £600 ($1,020), from the French jeweller Louis Gérard when she was officiating at a polo match. As the gift was from a business concern, rather than from a friend, she could not keep the ring. Instead it raised £7,000 ($11,900) for Birthright, one of the charities of which the Princess is patron.

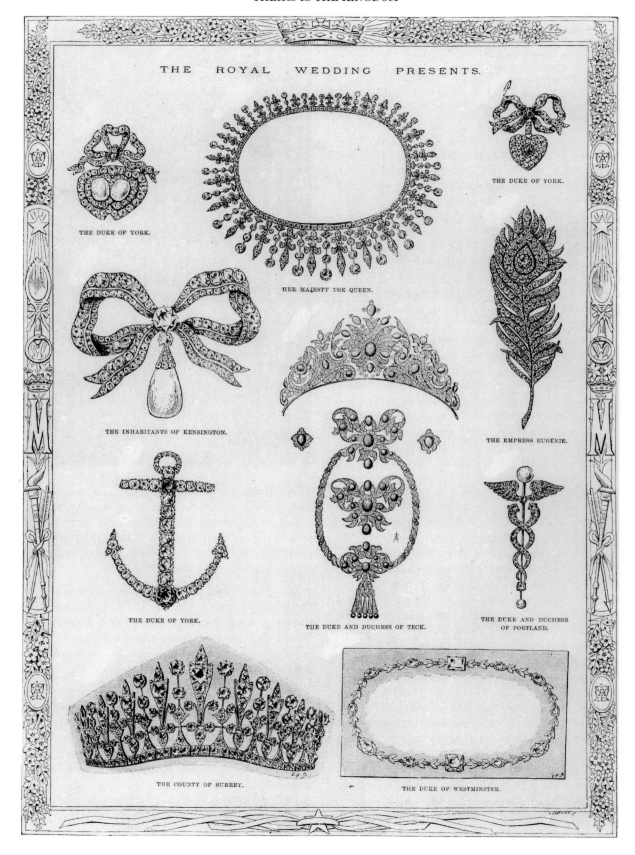

THE ROYAL WEDDING PRESENTS.

THE DUKE OF YORK.

HER MAJESTY THE QUEEN.

THE DUKE OF YORK.

THE INHABITANTS OF KENSINGTON.

THE EMPRESS EUGÉNIE.

THE DUKE OF YORK.

THE DUKE AND DUCHESS OF TECK.

THE DUKE AND DUCHESS
OF PORTLAND.

THE COUNTY OF SURREY.

THE DUKE OF WESTMINSTER.

LEFT: *Queen Mary's wedding presents included a diamond tiara from the county of Surrey.*

The constant stream of gifts becomes a flood during times of royal celebration. At the wedding of Princess May of Teck, later Queen Mary, ladies from various British towns presented their gifts at thirty minute intervals. When the Prince and Princess of Wales were married at St Paul's Cathedral in 1981 they were deluged with gifts. Even as a bachelor Prince Charles had a vision of what was to come. When he moved into Highgrove he didn't trouble to furnish the mansion, telling his staff, 'I'm bound to get lots of things when I marry.'

He was proved right. The Wales' homes at Kensington Palace and Highgrove are almost entirely decorated with affectionate tribute from around the world. The royal couple decided that Kensington Palace should be the repository for gifts from overseas countries — the glass bowl from the American people is on display in their hallway — while their country house would take more personal presents.

RIGHT and BELOW: *The Prince and Princess of Wales were inundated with wedding gifts, even accepting herbs for their garden at Highgrove.*

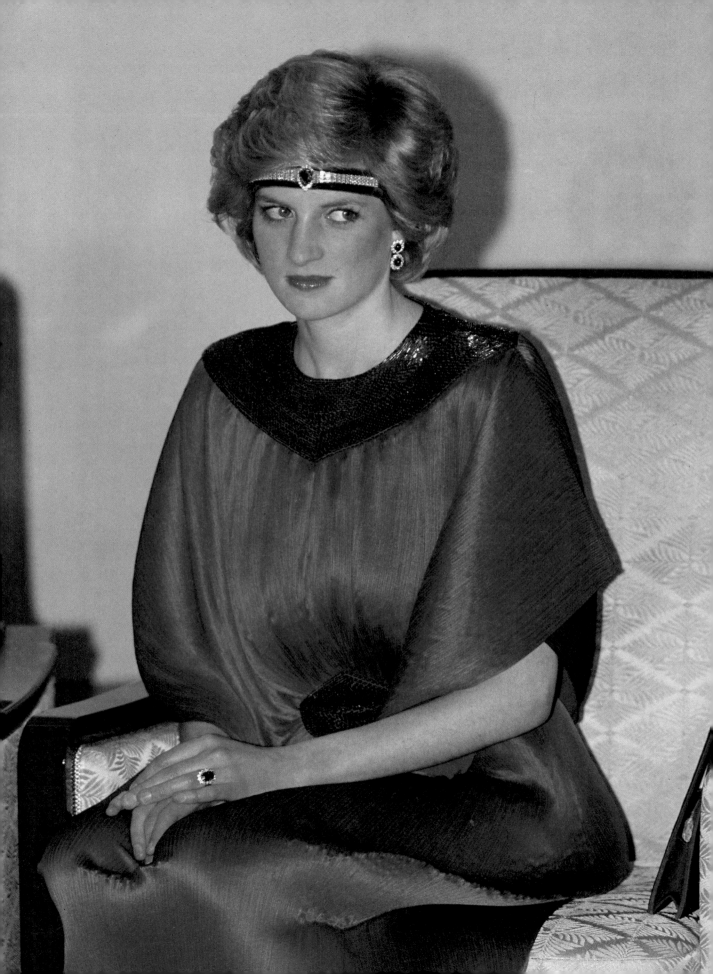

ABOVE LEFT: *Queen Mary's heirloom emerald necklace, which the Queen gave Diana as a wedding present, was used as a headband.* ABOVE RIGHT: *The Queen wearing Queen Mary's 'Girls of Great Britain and Ireland' tiara, her Dorset Bow brooch and necklace from the Nizam of Hyderabad.*
OPPOSITE: *The Princess of Wales also converted a wedding suite of sapphires from Saudi Arabia which she wore in Japan in 1986.*

Indeed, Highgrove is testimony to the generosity felt towards the future King and his Consort.

Their £10,000 ($23,000) dinner service was a gift from workers at the Waterford crystal factory, their wrought iron entrance gates were presented by the nearby town of Tetbury, their swimming pool was paid for by the Army, even the herbs and bulbs in their garden are from various women's associations and gardening groups, while they received so many kitchens that several were adapted for the homes of estate workers.

The real centrepieces of a royal wedding are the gifts of jewellery – those proud, often poignant fragments of history that spell continuity and succession. Prince Charles' wedding day was the occasion when his young bride, who had only ever worn a gold 'D' on a

neck chain, came into a glittering regal heritage which symbolized her transformation into a Princess. Her first great jewel – a tiara of lovers' knots of diamonds from which hang nineteen teardrop pearls – was a gift from the Queen who in turn had been given it by Queen Mary.

The Princess of Wales has proved that she is not a prisoner of the past, never treating her priceless gifts like untouchable museum pieces. She transformed a 14-inch long emerald Art Deco necklace, which was designed from the Cambridge emeralds and given to the Queen by Queen Mary, into a headband which she wore at a charity dance in Australia.

On her own wedding day the Queen received jewels from the Indian royal Houses, notably a rose-patterned diamond bandeau and necklace from the Nizam of Hyderabad. In changed political circumstances where oil is the language of power today, it was significant that it was the Gulf rulers who gave the most opulent presents to the Princess of Wales.

The Crown Prince of Saudi Arabia gave the Princess a magnificent £600,000 ($1,392,000) suite of sapphires comprising earrings, a ring, bracelet and a watch with seven sapphire

OPPOSITE: *The Spencer tiara, here worn in Bahrain, was the most important family heirloom Lady Diana brought with her into the House of Windsor.*

clusters all made by the London jewellers Asprey. In his memoirs Prince Charles' former valet, Stephen Barry, archly observed, 'I can confirm the figure, as we had it valued immediately. For insurance purposes of course.'

The Princess once again demonstrated her assured sense of style by converting the showy watch and the sapphire from the ring into a headband which she wore during an audience with Emperor Hirohito in Japan.

She regularly wears the chain with the diamond Prince of Wales pendant which the

BELOW: *The Queen wears the most expensive brooch in the world – the third and fourth parts of the mighty Cullinan diamond which was presented to Edward VII by the Transvaal Government. She calls the brooch 'granny's chips' and could sell it for at least £9.3 million ($15.8 million).*

Queen Mother gave her after the announcement of her engagement to the Prince of Wales. This oval pendant was a wedding gift to Princess Alexandra of Denmark, given in humility by the 'ladies of Bristol' in 1863. A perfect illustration of how tribute originally given to honour the public personage is now considered to be a private family heirloom.

Royal wedding gifts have traditionally been a show of splendour for subjects to admire. When Lady Elizabeth Bowes-Lyon married the young Duke of York in 1923, people fought and jostled to look at their presents, particularly her jewellery. She received a suite of diamonds and sapphires from Queen Mary, diamonds from her husband Bertie, a delicate tiara from her father, the Earl of Strathmore, while the citizens of London contributed towards a classical pearl chain.

Jewels have long been the true currency of majesty. They breathed overwhelming opulence and the certainty of social supremacy. As the historian of jewellery, Dr Joan Evans,

The royal sceptre with cross is one of the most ancient emblems of power. Charles II first used it for his Coronation in 1660. In 1911 George V added the largest of the Cullinan diamonds.

has observed, 'Jewellery . . . answers to the supersititious need for reinforcing human powers by things that seem to a savage more lasting and more mysterious than man.' Jewels have spoken an international language as they have made dramatic, romantic and often bloody transfers from one royal House to another. They are eminently practical – a fortune can be hidden in a handbag or sewn into a Duchess' hat. It is no coincidence that when the air raid sirens shattered the evening peace around Badminton, Queen Mary's wartime retreat, the first thing she reached for was the suitcase containing the best of her fabulous collection.

Jewels have been the stuff of royal wills down the centuries, their regal owners carefully alloting their fortune of 'chips'. When Henry VIII's fourth wife, Anne of Cleves, died in 1557, the content of her will was almost entirely devoted to the distribution of her jewellery. 'We give to the Duke of Cleves our brother a ring of gold with a fair diamond, and to our sister, the Duchess of Cleves, his wife, a ring, having therein a great rock ruby, the ring being black enamelled. We give to our sister, the Lady Emely, a ring of gold having therein a fair pointed diamond. And to the Lady Katherine, Duchess of Suffolk, a ring of gold, haveing a fair table diamond, somewhat long . . . To Queen Mary, our best jewel . . . To the Lady Elizabeth, my second best jewel.'

Indeed jewels were the first royal possessions to be separated from Crown property. In her will of 1566 the ill-fated Mary Queen of Scots made a clear distinction between the Honours of Scotland (the Scottish Crown Jewels) and her personal pieces. A little over 250 years later when Queen Victoria ascended the throne her inheritance was threadbare, squandered by the Hanovers and their predecessors. The diamonds in the famous Shamrock Crown of George IV were rented – a fact that Queen Victoria remedied during her reign – while previous coronations were marred by haggling over the hire costs of regalia.

OPPOSITE: *The Queen Mother's Coronation Crown which includes the fabulous 108-carat 'Koh-i-Nor' diamond. This stone, which forms part of the Crown Jewels, brings bad luck on male owners.*

106

ABOVE: *The actual size of the Star of Africa and the 2nd Star of Africa which were the first cleavings from the huge Cullinan diamond and now form part of the Crown Jewels. When Joseph Asscher successfully cut the stone he fainted.*

However, her own expenditure was small compared to the seaborne riches which travelled to Britain from Bombay and the Cape. Cases, chests and trunks filled with priceless jewels made their way to the heart of the Empire from a land where elephants had anklets of solid gold, where they played marbles with emeralds, where the 162-carat Jacob diamond was used as a paperweight and where 21-gun salutes were fired from golden cannon. Even today the elderly descendants of the Nizam of Hyderabad, now living in London, recall the unguarded Gold Vault at the Palace which was left to gather dust. The Nizam reasoned that the identity of any thief would be betrayed by the shape of his footprints. They remember the story of one of the Nizam's wives who had a duck egg ruby that shone with such brilliance that it served as a bedside lamp. This was India, the jewel in Victoria's crown.

Her affection for the mysterious East was kindled when she was presented with the fabled Koh-i-noor diamond by the East India Company in 1850. The stone, which was confiscated from the Maharajah of Lahore, was accepted not as a personal gift but as 'belonging to the Crown and to be worn by all future queens in the right of it'. These were jewels brought by conquest. For the most part her fabulous offerings were the *nazar*, or tribute, from the royal Houses of India.

The Queen guarded her colonial jewel jealously but in 1875, with much reluctance, she allowed her eldest son, the future Edward VII, to make a six-month visit. It was an uproarious, decadent progress through the various states, bagging tigers, shooting elephants and quaffing champagne, and the Prince came home loaded down with gifts and a veritable zoo of animals, stuffed and living. A silver bathtub, a gold bed, gold crowns hung with emeralds, gold and silver swords, a diamond brooch for Princess Alexandra, and a pearl necklace with an emerald pendant set in gold for the Queen were among the gifts presented.

In return he gave gold snuff boxes and signed photographs. (Little has changed in 100 years. The Queen now gives photographs and cuff links. 'I am afraid this is rather small,' she will say.) However, the Indian princes were displeased with constant reports implying that gifts of 'equal value' had been exchanged as Lord Suffield made clear in his memoirs of the visit. He wrote:

The legal battle with the Elector of Hanover for the disputed fortune left by Queen Charlotte was not just over a principle but also for a goodly portion of her inheritance – a treasure chest Queen Victoria could ill-afford to lose. Yet during her sixty-year reign she amassed a fortune in jewels by purchase and tribute. She spent a total of £158,887 ($794,435) with Garrard – around £8 million ($13.6 million) at today's prices – on diamonds, sapphires, and her favourites, blood red rubies. They were for private gifts, State presents, imperial crowns and family keepsakes – but most of all they were for the private royal collection.

ABOVE: *Royal ladies are usually given jewellery for launching a ship. The Princess Royal was given this diamond tiara when she launched a 250,000-ton tanker for a Hong Kong shipping magnate.*

The Indian Princes expressed much annoyance that any comparison should have been made between their gifts and the Prince's. We took with us £40,000 ($200,000) worth of presents, beautiful and well-chosen. But so generous were the Rajahs that it was with some little difficulty that they were persuaded to limit the value of their gifts.

The royal ships, *HMS Osborne* and *HMS Serapis*, were loaded down with their cargo of emeralds, sapphires, rubies, a serpent bracelet -- which the present Queen thinks rather spooky — gold drinking cups, silver plate and diamond-encrusted armour. In total three leather trunks were loaded into the strongroom filled with priceless jewellery. As Lord Suffield recorded, 'Of material things we took a cargo worth a king's ransom. The gifts made to the Prince were quite beyond valuation.'

The Queen's plump, eager fingers could barely hold the ruby necklaces, the pearls and the diamonds as she dipped into the chests which her eldest son proudly set before her. As the Prince basked in the glory of Empire, the Prime Minister, Benjamin Disraeli, made a grateful Queen the Empress of India — Victoria

Regina et Imperatrix. At a banquet at Windsor Castle to celebrate the event the new Queen Empress greeted her guests smothered in jewels, many from her Indian majarajahs. Disraeli, now elevated to Lord Beaconsfield, marvelled at the change in a sovereign who had hitherto appeared in the stark onyx and ivory of mourning. She teased him further by sending a servant to fetch three large leather cases from the vaults. Each one was brimful of wondrous jewellery from the East.

The fruits of Empire continued to flow in throughout her reign, particularly during her Diamond Jubilee Year in 1897, as the rulers and people of the colonies and beyond sent their 'humble offerings' to Queen Victoria who was worshipped from afar as their 'Great White Goddess'.

When she died, five moroccan leather Gladstone bags contained the twinkling harvest of the first Empress in the nation's history. However, these paled when placed against the festival of jewels paraded at the Court of St Petersburg in Russia. Every Christmas the Windsors were reminded of the riches of their Imperial royal cousins when the Princess of Wales's sister, the Empress of Russia, sent ropes of pearls, rich red rubies and amusing Fabergé trinkets for their pleasure and delight.

Yet within twenty years of Queen Victoria's death, the Imperial family had been murdered by the Bolsheviks and Queen Mary's eyes caressed the jewels of a once-proud Empire.

It was said of her that no other woman in Europe could wear so many jewels with such easy assurance and perfect poise. 'Like addressing St Paul's,' said the smart Society diarist, Chips Channon. Jewels were her craving and her delight, an outlet for her frustrated creativity. Her critics said she lavished more love on her collections than on her six unhappy children. It is noticeable that in her famous Doll's House the jewel vault is bigger than the nursery and that, apart from the occasional guard, the mansion is bereft of life. Those friends still living say that she was a warmer, more approachable Consort than her biographers would have us believe. If that is true then Queen Mary is a classic case of the sublimation of self for the impersonal symbolism of royalty.

She showed her mettle when she retrieved the famous Cambridge heirlooms her brother Prince Frank had so foolishly given away. A year later she demonstrated her iron control

and stern-eyed splendour before 80,000 subjects as she and King George V accepted the homage of the Indian rulers at the Delhi Durbar of 1911. 'The jewel you have given me will ever be very precious in my eyes, and, whenever I wear it, though thousands of miles of land and sea separate us, my thoughts will fly to the homes of India and create again and again this happy meeting,' the Queen told the 'Ladies of India' after they presented her with a necklace and brooch which now form part of the stunning Cambridge and Delhi Durbar parure.

OPPOSITE: *The stunning Cambridge and Delhi Durbar parure forms a magnificent part of the Queen's collection. It is made from the Cambridge emeralds inherited by Queen Mary, gifts of emeralds from the Delhi Durbar and cleavings from the Cullinan diamond. Its history symbolizes the combination of family fortune and public tribute that is the hallmark of the dynasty.*
BELOW: *Scene from the 1911 Delhi Durbar where George V wore the Indian Crown.*

Those days of innocent imperialism were shattered forever by the carnage of the First World War. Making his way through war-torn Europe was an unlikely English adventurer, Bertie Stopford, clutching two battered Gladstone bags. Inside, wrapped in yellowing newspaper, were emeralds, pearls and rubies together with diamond tiaras – the hidden treasure of Grand Duchess Vladimar. The Duchess, in hiding in Switzerland following the Russian Revolution, had pleaded with Stopford to recover the family jewels from a walled safe inside the now looted Vladimir Palace in St Petersburg. Legend has it that he disguised himself as an old woman and hid the tiara in the lining of his black bonnet, cramming the pearls into cherries which were sown on as trimmings. Others say he dressed as a workman and made his way to safety through the British Embassy. The Grand Duchess had little time to renew acquaintance with her collection. She died in 1920 and a year later these romantic jewels came up for sale.

With Europe awash with treasures from a dozen toppled monarchies, Queen Mary made a number of shrewd purchases, paying a rock bottom price for the Grand Duchess Vladimir's favourite piece, the interlaced ovals of diamonds with suspended pendant pearls. However, her greatest coup came nearly a decade later with the death of the Dowager Empress Marie Feodorovna, the mother of the murdered Tsar. She had escaped the massacre of the Romanov royal family and, after seeking protection behind the White Army for several years, eventually returned to her native Denmark. The impecunious old lady, who was used to unheard-of wealth, settled uneasily to the straitened circumstances of the Danish court. She was the quintessential royal, not understanding the value of money but having no difficulty in spending it. Her daughter, Grand Duchess Xenia, became the laughing stock of European society by naively allowing a pair of scoundrels to trick her out of her matchless collection of pearls.

George V took pity on his unworldly royal cousins, lending Xenia and her sister, Grand Duchess Olga, Frogmore Cottage in the grounds of Windsor Park and settling a £2,400-a-year ($11,664) pension on them. As the incorrigible Empress lapsed into senility and sickness there were fears that her jewels — the bedridden old lady never let the suitcase containing her family collection out of her sight — would be spirited away by a dark conspiracy of crooks and communists.

Shortly before the Empress died in 1928, George V convinced the Empress's daughters that the safest place for the jewels would be in Britain where they could be assessed and sold, and the proceeds used to secure their future. The jewels, sealed in a leather trunk, were deposited in the vault at Buckingham Palace. When the trunk yielded its contents even

ABOVE: *The Queen Mother with Prince Charles at the Coronation in 1953. The three-row festoon necklace of 105 diamonds was George VI's idea.*

the normally matter-of-fact Sir Frederick Ponsonby, Keeper of the Privy Purse, was taken aback by the glittering reality of these fabled stones. He recalled in his memoirs,

Ropes of the most wonderful pearls were taken out, all graduated, the largest being the size of a big cherry. Cabochon emeralds and large rubies and sapphires were laid out. I then retired discreetly from the room.

The representative from the jewellers, Hennell and Sons, who had agreed to sell the stones, immediately offered the sisters £100,000 ($486,000) on account until they were sold. Here the plot, already ripe with intrigue, thickens. According to Ponsonby, the jewels raised £350,000 ($1.7 million) which was put in trust by the King for the two sisters. Naturally Queen Mary bought a number of the pieces, which have now been passed on to various members of the royal family, including the Queen Mother and Princess Margaret. This story contradicts the version advanced by the aggrieved Russan royal family.

ABOVE: *The King George IV State diadem which the Queen inherited from her father. It is worn to and from the State Opening of Parliament seen by millions of people every year.*

Grand Duchess Olga, who died in a squalid flat above a baker's shop in Toronto, Canada, always claimed that she and her sister never received their full share of the sorry spoils of the Romanov dynasty. Their evidence was contained in papers which showed that Queen Mary had held on to the jewels until 1933 – the height of the Depression – and then offered them a mere £60,000 ($291,600).

It is undeniable that in just twenty-five years Queen Mary had amassed an unsurpassed collection of jewels that left the present Queen overwhelmed by her awesome inheritance. On the night before she died, Queen Mary paid her own tribute to the nation which had filled her caskets. She had a book read to her about India and she paraphrased Mary Tudor's famous dying remark by saying that India would be forever engraved on her heart.

The tribute of tiaras, the gifts of brooches, pins and earrings has continued to flow unabated. A diamond brooch for Princess Elizabeth when she launched her first ship, HMS

OPPOSITE: *The Queen Mother wearing the tiara she had made from South African diamonds, with her corgi Ranger.* ABOVE: *Princess Margaret's tiara was bought from Lord Poltimore in 1959 for around £5,000 ($8,500). She wore it on her wedding day.*

Vanguard, in 1944 was but the first of many such gifts.

The mines of southern Africa have been generous and, long after King Edward VII accepted the mighty cleavings from the Cullinan diamond in 1907 have yielded her 'best diamonds', the pale pink Williamson stones and blue white diamonds from the Kimberley mines.

The Indian majarajahs are no more. Instead there have been pearl chokers from Kuwait, an aquamarine bracelet from Brazil and sapphires from the Emperor of Japan.

How much is this fabulous collection worth? The Queen's heritage has never been professionally valued, jewellers shrugging off the task by arguing that the historical provenance of the stones would make it an academic exercise. The collection is literally priceless. Nevertheless everything, even jewels owned by the House of Windsor, has a price. In 1901 Queen Victoria's collection was estimated to be worth around £5 million ($24.2 million). How much can the jewels have increased in value?

In 1989 Laurence Krashes, an appraiser for Harry Winston in New York for more than sixteen years and author of *Harry Winston: The Ultimate Jeweller*, agreed to give the first-ever professional appraisal of the Queen's personal collection for this book. It was based on the criteria that the collection would be assessed on their value as jewels and not their historical worth.

He examined the precious stones that make up the tiaras, brooches, earrings, necklaces, bracelets, pendants, watches and rings in the Sovereign's collection. Their purity and age was difficult to gauge as, unlike most other important collections such as the Crown Jewels of Iran, the Queen has not allowed a proper study of her glittering heritage. However, the critical factor was the 'cut' of the jewels. Most of the Queen's diamonds were 'old cuts' which would need reworking if they were to be marketable. That factor alone considerably reduced their value as they would lose numerous carats if they were reshaped for modern settings.

His estimate is that the Queen's *known* jewels would realize between £36,000,000 ($61.2 million) and £42,000,000 ($71.4 million). The Queen Mother's jewels, including her tiaras and brooches, are worth around £3,500,000 ($5,950,000), while the Princess of Wales, who is already starting to set fashion trends in jewellery, has a small collection worth around £2 million ($3.4 million).

Laurence Krashes says:

I treated the jewels as if they were owned by Mrs Joelene Casper from Tennessee not the Queen of England. This valuation is basically a guide into unknown territory. There are many pieces that have not been seen since the days of Queen Mary. No one knows for certain whether they have been broken up or are simply lying in vaults somewhere.

This is the greatest known private collection of historical jewels in the world. Yet it is not the most valuable. It is outranked by several other collections, notably those of the Sultan of Brunei, the Saudi Arabian royal family, the Iranian Treasury and the Sultanates of Oman and Qatar.

You have to remember that they have been actively buying huge quantities of new cut stones for the last forty years. The Sultan of Brunei alone bought a number of stones for $10 million each. There are also collections in India, hidden in numerous palaces and safes, that no one has ever seen and yet are simply fabulous.

However, worth is not necessarily value. A Saudi princess who sold her jewels would have them assessed on the basis of the stones. The Princess of Wales' jewels would be valued in the light of their association with the House of Windsor.

It is perhaps appropriate that Mr Krashes gives one of the highest values to tribute which the Queen received in her wedding year in 1947, a sign of the sinuous thread of homage extending from the days of Queen Victoria. The Williamson pink diamond flower brooch, worth around £2,353,000 ($4 million) at today's prices, was presented to Princess Elizabeth six months after her tour of South Africa in 1947. This 23-carat pink diamond, the world's most perfect specimen, was discovered by Dr John T. Williamson, an eccentric Canadian whose diamond mine in Tanzania was so productive that it gave him an income of £2 million ($7.7 million) a year in the 1940s.

He was a fanatical monarchist who derived immense pleasure from lavishing tribute on the royal House.

In all, Mr Krashes judges the Queen's known diamonds to be worth around £22,875,000 ($38.9 million). 'My estimate is conservative because of the old fashioned settings and cuts of the stones,' he explained. For example, the necklace the Queen calls 'my best diamonds' – a twenty-first birthday gift from the South African Government – is worth about £662,000 ($1,125 million), while the Queen Victoria collet diamond necklace and earrings would fetch around £1,176,000 (£2 million).

The Queen's collection of emeralds, including the magnificent Cambridge and Delhi Durbar parure, is worth around £5,750,000 ($9,775,000), while her pearls – her favourite jewels – would reach around £3,265,000 ($5,555,000) on the open market. Add to that her sapphires, worth more than £1,420,000 ($2.41 million) and her Burmese rubies, including the intricate Queen Mary, Rose of York bracelet, which are valued at more than £1,350,000 ($2.3 million) and the Queen's fortune in jewels becomes apparent.

ABOVE LEFT: *The wheat ear brooches were ordered by William IV in 1830 and have been in the family ever since.* ABOVE RIGHT: *A rare glimpse of the Crown amethysts, originally owned by Queen Victoria's mother, the Duchess of Kent.* OPPOSITE: *The President and People of Brazil gave the Queen a number of aquamarines she later made into this tiara.*

This estimate is based on the jewels which are known and have been photographed. Yet the vault at Buckingham Palace is filled with rings, brooches and pendants of an Edwardian and Victorian design which have barely seen the light of day.

There are at least three tiaras from Queen Mary's collection in store while mystery surrounds the dramatic diamond tiara with emerald spikes which she wore at the Delhi Durbar of 1911. It was last worn in 1947 by Queen Elizabeth, now the Queen Mother. What, too, of the black opal Queen Mary bought from the Australian Pavilion at the Wembley exhibition in 1925 or the fine emeralds sent to Queen Victoria in 1842 by the Imam of Muscat? 'A trifling gift scarcely worth being mentioned,' he wrote as he sent her 'two pearl necklaces, two emeralds . . . and ten cashmere shawls'.

The ruby brooch and pendant that passed to Queen Mary from Countess Torby in her will have not been seen since they formed the chief jewels in a portrait of the Queen by David Jagger in 1932. Were these jewels, stored in the vaults, broken down and reset to form the stones for the Duchess of York's engagement ring?

Mr Krashes' expert estimate of the private royal jewels, must be taken in the context that the jewels we see are but the tip of an iceberg buried deep in the bowels of Buckingham Palace. At the same time the royal associations would add a tremendous premium to the estimate. Here there is a recent precedent in the auction in Geneva of the Duchess of Windsor's stylish jewellery collection. Christie's expected it to fetch between £3 and £5 million ($5.1–8.5 million). In the event it realized £31,500,000 ($53.55 million) amidst scenes of frenzied buying as the international jet set, including Joan Collins and Elizabeth Taylor, attempted to purchase a piece of history.

If the Queen did decide to sell her jewellery, it would go under the hammer for at least £300 million ($510 million). Those who claim that the royal family never sell their heritage of jewellery should bear in mind the night that Princess Michael of Kent prepared to attend a glittering royal function. As she headed for the door of her apartment at Kensington Palace there was consternation as a diamond from her tiara fell to the floor. Her butler lead the search but then to his horror felt a crunch under his shoe.

He had crushed the diamond under foot. It was paste. The Princess had discreetly sold many of the originals which she had inherited from her mother-in-law, Princess Marina of Kent, who in turn had been given superb suites of jewels on her wedding day and was presented with her tiara by the indomitable Queen Mary.

In 1965 when George VI's sister, the Princess Royal, died her estate, including her jewellery collection, was auctioned at Christie's to pay death duties. While Queen Mary's daughter willed the finest pieces – including a sapphire tiara of Queen Victoria's – to the royal family, there were still 138 separate pieces of jewellery for sale. Her collection raised £52,852 ($148,000) – including £12,500 ($35,000) paid by Harry Winston for a sapphire necklace.

These jewels, once tribute to the Sovereign, pass down through the family and, when their

origin is all but forgotten, they are occasionally privately disposed of. However, does the Queen have the right to sell this historic collection? The answer is yes – although she has never been inclined to do so. The Queen and her family own the vast majority of their jewels seen in public. They are in no sense State property like, for example, Buckingham Palace or Windsor Castle.

While the Crown Jewels, kept in the Tower of London and brought out for Coronations and the State Opening of Parliament, are, in the ringing words of Lord Cobbold, 'vested in the Sovereign and therefore inalienable', much of the rest of the collection is personal property.

Over the last 150 years certain jewels like the Koh-i-noor and the largest of the Cullinan diamonds have been accepted by the Sovereign on behalf of the nation. This Crown Jewellery – as opposed to the 'Crown Jewels' – is over-shadowed by the collection amassed by the House of Windsor. As far as the Crown Jewellery is concerned the Queen considers these to be family heirlooms and does not, according to Lord Cobbold, 'regard any of these items as being at her free personal disposal'.

Nowhere is the ambivalent relationship between gifts accepted by the royal family on behalf of the nation and for the dynasty demonstrated than with the history of the fabled Cullinan diamond. The stone was presented to Edward VII in 1907 as a peace offering by the Transvaal Government following the bitter Boer War.

Edward VII announced that he would accept this magnificent gift 'for myself and successors' and said that he would arrange that 'this great and unique diamond be kept and preserved among the historic jewels which form the heirlooms of the Crown.'

The cutting of the stone produced two principal stones, the Cullinan I, now called the Greater Star of Africa, which was set in the head of the Sceptre with the Cross and the Cullinan II which was mounted at the front of the Imperial State Crown. These are now on display at the Tower of London and form part of the Crown Jewels.

Further cleavings of the diamond produced nine major stones known as the 'chips'. They

ABOVE: *Princess Michael of Kent inherited this spiked tiara from Princess Marina of Greece.*
OPPOSITE: *Princess Marina wearing part of a superb sapphire and diamond parure from Queen Mary for this elegant Beaton portrait.*

were given as the fee to Dutch diamond company of Messrs I. J. Asscher who undertook the daunting task of cutting the stone. However, Edward VII now bought the marquise cut stone, the sixth Cullinan chip, and gave it to Queen Alexandra. In 1910 the South African purchased the remaining chips from Asscher and presented them to Queen Mary, hence the Queen's phrase 'granny's chips' in reference to these fabulous family heirlooms.

Thus while Edward VII initially accepted the diamond on behalf of the Sovereign, and hence the nation, within four years a substantial part of the Cullinan diamond was privately held by the Windsors. The Cullinan stones are the

single most generous offering ever accepted by the House of Windsor and a stunning addition to their fortune. Simply valued as stones and disregarding their historic provenance they are worth at least £10,835,000 ($18,420,000). The brooch made up of the Cullinan III and IV is the most expensive in the world, valued by Laurence Krashes, at £9.3 million ($15.8 million).

Hence, the majority of the jewels are owned outright by the Queen and her family – a fact which is emphasized by the way the jewels are preserved and administered.

The Queen's private jewels are fiercely guarded by her formidable dresser, the octogenarian Scotswoman, Bobo MacDonald, who has served the Queen since 1926 and who has the key to the battered leather pouches and cases that house her favourite 'working' jewels. Furthermore, it is the Queen who personally pays Garrard should anything in her collection need to be altered or cleaned.

Contrast this with the Queen's collection of pictures which are national treasures, restored and preserved by experts employed by the Department of Environment, even though they are privately administered by the Queen's representative, the Surveyor of the Queen's Pictures. There is no comparable post for the jewellery within the Royal Household. The Queen keeps a close watch over her treasures.

The important difference between the Queen's jewellery and her picture collection is that she has not sold an important picture during her reign, while family jewellery has been auctioned or sold privately.

At the same time, it is a personal collection of jewellery which is regulated by several unwritten rules. It is noticeable that the tribute accumulated over the years is treated differently from gifts offered by friendship, marriage or will. The latter are the royal family's property which they can distribute how they wish, while the former may be reset or altered but must not leave the Sovereign's immediate family. Tact and diplomacy decree that tribute accepted on official visits may ultimately be personal

property but, because of the formal nature of the tour, these gifts must be treated as if they were Crown property.

When the Prince and Princess of Wales visited the Gulf States in 1989, gifts of jewellery were presented to the royal couple by their Arab hosts, proof of the continuing tribute honouring the House of Windsor.

It is an endless river that will ultimately make the Princess of Wales heir to the greatest private jewellery collection in the world. On her tours and visits the Princess is building her own collection of jewels, a testimony to the continuing mystique of monarchy.

How much will her gifts to be worth? No one will really know for certain for some time – except perhaps Amit Roy.

4
Monarch of the Glen

In summer soft clinging mists swirl down from the heather-covered hills while in a hard winter the roads can be closed by snow for weeks. This is Balmoral, perhaps the last royal kingdom. A pocket principality where due deference and loyalty is still shown to the laird of the manor and the one place where the Queen is monarch of all she surveys. Balmoral is truly the Windsor family seat, a fact reinforced by the Queen Mother's Scottish ancestry and homes.

Traditionally, the royal working life means that every move is watched and photographed. 'Zoo teas,' the Queen Mother calls the garden

parties at Buckingham Palace when 4,000 heads swivel to watch the royal family chatter and consume their cucumber sandwiches.

Even at social events like Royal Ascot and the Derby, the Queen is on permanent display. As her former Private Secretary Lord Adeane recorded, 'The Queen, who can never enjoy these engagements with the freedom of a holiday maker, the pleasure of attending them is bound to be tempered by the strain imposed on her as a public figure and by the knowledge that somebody is looking at her all the time and that she is being continually photographed and televised as well.'

However, at Balmoral, even more than Sandringham, she and her family enjoy long days of peace and privacy. It is respected by the local people who give short shrift to Fleet Street photographers who try to spoil the tranquility.

OPPOSITE: *The Queen and the Duke of Edinburgh in the drawing-room at Balmoral, her Scottish home.* BELOW: *As monarch of the glen, the Queen exerts effortless authority over her domain.*

When the Queen is in residence, the local bakers in Ballater, G. Leith and Son, make sure that they have a large supply of the Selkirk Bannoch ('a good big bun', they say with some satisfaction). Over the road is the local chemist, J. and D. Murray whose most popular preparation, Ironside's Emollient Skin Cream, was a favourite with George VI. Occasionally the Queen, dressed in a Hermes headscarf, will undertake a little unobtrusive shopping in the town, frequenting H. M. Sheridan, the local butcher.

Like all the locals, the shopkeepers are discreet, traditional and quirkily loyal. For example, the local newsagent recently displayed a copy of the banned book, *Spycatcher*, in his window. He refused all entreaties to part with it but left it there all summer as both a mute protest against the Government and, one can only suppose, as a silent entreaty to the Queen. The assumption being that she would see the book, appreciate the protest, and make her own feelings known to Mrs Thatcher when she came to visit. Here the Queen is seen as the local squire who may help to redress wrongs and grievances.

Both she and the Queen Mother, her face a picture of amused eagerness, are the regular guests of honour at the biennial Crathie Sale of Work organised by the local women. They walk round the stalls selling home-made cakes and jams and admire the locally grown potted plants and knitted pullovers – the Ladies from the Big House among their subjects.

The Balmoral estate has been in the hands of the Windsors for almost as long as the dynasty has been in existence. Queen Victoria bought the land sight unseen in 1848. She was charmed by the granite mansion where, on the first evening of her occupation, red deer grazed outside her window. She and Prince Albert developed the estate, initiating a huge, well organized building scheme including a ballroom for the newly dedicated baronial mansion and a distillery. Following Prince Albert's death in 1861, her Scottish home became a shrine to her dead husband although she continued with his plans to develop the land.

While she loved the remote home this feeling was not shared by the Prince of Wales, later King Edward VII, who frequently grumbled

BELOW: *George Smith and Co, based in Ballater, supply fishing tackle to Prince Charles.*
OPPOSITE: *The Queen at her ease on her Deeside estate where she spends every summer holiday.*

about the turreted baronial mansion, calling it a 'Highland barn with 1,000 draughts'. Even the purchase of nearby Birkhall Lodge, now the home of the Queen Mother, could not tempt the Prince of Wales.

However, her grandson, George V, shared her enthusiasm and it was always with a sense of homecoming that the King stepped down from the royal train at Ballater, inspected a guard of honour drawn from a Scottish regiment and then drove to his home. 'Glad to be in this dear place again after six years,' he wrote in August 1919, 'and to see all our nice people again.'

Like Queen Victoria, he warmed to their independence and direct, plain speech. As he shrugged off the cares of the world from his shoulders, he became jocund and almost carefree. 'And what is your name?' he asked the granddaughter of a shooting friend. 'I am Ann Peace Arabella Mackintosh of Mackintosh,' the King was solemnly informed. 'Ah,' replied the King, humbly, 'I'm just plain George.'

BDLOW: Prince Charles with his pet Labrador, Harvey goes for a day's salmon fishing by the river Dee. RIGHT: The Queen, who has never been seen fishing, with Prince Philip in the tackle room at Balmoral.

This mood of jovial informality is seen most clearly at the annual Servants', or Gillies', Ball. During Queen Victoria's day they were drunken affairs with servants collapsing in the ballroom and the Queen herself whisked off her feet by kilted gillies as the pipes whirled and skirled into the early hours.

The present Balls may be rather more decorous but they are still unsophisticated, time honoured and full of gaiety. It is a traditional scene of tartans and taffeta, of pipers and claymores and where nervous farm hands finger their outsize collars in apprehension of being called to the royal presence. At the dance itself the Queen's Pipe Major always walks over to the prospective dance partner after the Queen has made her choice. When the Queen does pick an unpractised dancer to accompany her onto the floor, she indicates to the bandleader to slow down the pace. She may be above criticism but she is not immune to heavy, unpractised feet treading on her toes.

At both Sandringham and Balmoral the royal family are able to relax away from prying eyes. Edward VII organized tricycle races in the ballroom and the grand staircase was often converted into a carpeted toboggan run with a large silver tray as the sledge. Artless jokes like

making apple pie beds, dusting pillows with talcum powder and leaving dead birds beneath the sheets were – and are – habitual pranks. Once a guest released a bear called Charlie from his pit much to everyone's consternation. Ever since his demise he has remained a source of terror. His stuffed and mounted form is often placed in the lift to scare members of staff at the end of a long night.

One one occasion a drunken, sleeping servant was carried, bed and all, into the Balmoral dining-room shortly before breakfast. The Queen and the Duke of Edinburgh calmly ate their toast and marmalade as the servant, serene in his stupor, slept on. Traditionally, the Highland holiday is the time when the Queen presents her long-service medals to her staff. As an aged retainer, resplendent in his scarlet uniform, prepared to accept his Royal Victorian Order a flour bomb caught him on the side of his head and ruined his pristine splendour. The Duke of York helped catch the culprit who was bundled into a wicker hamper basket and thrown into the River Dee. He has also been known to hide thistles in his elder brother's bed while the normally no-nonsense Princess Royal has been known to leave plastic spiders in staff bedrooms.

While the pace of life at Balmoral is more relaxed than at Buckingham Palace or Windsor Castle, protocol is still preserved. Queen Victoria strictly controlled her Household and would decide their precise time of arrival and departure and direct that they must never leave the house until she herself had gone out. When they did leave they could only use ponies, divided into five categories, assigned to them. If anyone happened to cross the Queen's path when she went for a walk they were obliged to hide behind a bush.

It was no less formal during George V's reign. When he dined with Queen Mary he would wear his kilt and Order of the Thistle, attended by eight footmen and five pipers. For picnics on the shore of the brooding Loch Muick, a convoy of claret-coloured Daimlers with gold-plated radiators would wind along the single track road. The food was served by footmen and cooked by a chef in a white hat. Today the Duke of Edinburgh is the master of ceremonies and it

RIGHT: *The Queen and the Duke of Edinburgh have done much to revitalize and modernize the 20,000-acre Sandringham estate in Norfolk.*

134

is Prince Charles' boast that he learned his own barbequing expertise by watching his father.

Balmoral is also very much a productive estate which the present Queen has done much to improve. Today the estate comprises some 43,000 acres, in addition to 7,600 acres of top-quality grouse moor at Delnadamph which she bought in 1977 for over £700,000 ($1.61 million). The policy of expansion, started by Prince Albert, has continued with some vigour in the present reign. In 1966 the Queen began a five-year programme of taking over farms whose tenancies had fallen vacant, enabling a fourfold increase in arable yield which has in turn reduced the cost of buying winter feed for her livestock.

The red deer which once grazed so peaceably under the windows of Balmoral Castle are now commercially farmed and the estate rears stalking ponies, including stock descended from two Haflinger brood mares given to the Queen by the Austrian President during a State visit in 1969.

Every morning, come hail or shine, the Queen, here with Prince Edward and guest, rides over her estate. Surprisingly in these safety conscious days she never wears a riding hat.

Both the Duke of Edinburgh, the driving force in royal modernization, and Prince Charles spend time in administering the estate and are fiercely protective of their boundaries and their privacy. In the past the Duke has tried to discourage ramblers from walking across the royal estate by replacing the 'Do Not Trespass' signs with ones which read 'Danger – Poisonous Adders'.

On one legendary occasion father and son had spent several hours hunting a stag, skilfully remaining downwind of the beast so that he would not scent them. At the very moment the Duke prepared to shoot, a young man, haversack slung over his shoulder, marched into view and innocently scared off the beast.

The Duke broke his cover and launched into an angry tirade at the bemused teenager. 'What the hell do you think you are doing?' exploded the Duke. However, the young man's stuttered reply silenced his guns. 'I'm doing this hike as part of my Duke of Edinburgh award scheme,' he said plaintively.

The sport of stag hunting comprises much of the Balmoral estate's value. At today's prices a red deer stag has a capital value of £15,000 ($25,500), each salmon on the Dee is valued at £5,000 ($9,500) when calculating fishing

The drawing-room at Sandringham has an air of faded grandeur which surprises visitors.

rights, while the grouse alone are worth between £7 and £10 million ($11.9–17 million). In recent years land prices have picked up from a low point of between £200 ($340) and £300 ($510) an acre. Arable land currently sells for between £600 ($1,020) and £1,000 ($1,700) an acre depending on its quality. If the Queen ever decides to sell her Highland estate, local estate agents estimate that it would be worth around £40 million ($68 million) – including £5 million ($9.5 million) for the mansion and the extensive gardens.

The valuations of the various royal estates, including Balmoral and Sandringham, were compiled from three main sources. Official documents such as the 'Report of the Comptroller of the Auditor General of the Crown Estates' 1988 and annual accounts from the Duchies of Lancaster and Cornwall provided much basic information, while the Inland Revenue's Property Market Report, which values land by type and situation, gave an

accurate indication of the worth of other royal holdings. At the same time local estate agents and surveyors were consulted for their professional appraisals of the royal land. It was from these three sources that an assessment of the value of the royal estates was compiled.

Ironically Balmoral, which has never been the white elephant that Sandringham once was, is worth much less than the Queen's 20,000 acres in low-lying Norfolk. Sandringham's good-quality arable land means that the estate is worth around £60 million ($102 million) while the 274-roomed House and gardens, renovated during the 1960s and 1970s, would sell for around £15 million ($25.5 million) today.

Edward VII, as Prince of Wales, loved his Norfolk retreat but an extensive rebuilding programme soon drained all the savings made from his income from the Duchy of Cornwall. He saw it not only as a focus for leisured splendour but also as a profitable farming

OVERLEAF: *If the Queen ever sold Sandringham it would raise around £60 million ($102 million).*

enterprise, quickly establishing three major herds of pedigree cattle, a flock of pedigree sheep and two studs of world famous Shire and Hackney horses. Queen Alexandra even maintained her own farm in which every animal had to be pure white in colouring.

However, in some quarters Edward VII was vilified as one who cared more for the welfare of his pheasants and partridges than his tenants, while George V's own ideas of moral welfare, closing down the public houses during the First World War and replacing them with teetotal village clubs, scarcely endeared him to farm workers.

Nevertheless both monarchs enjoyed their role as squire, paying their workers well, regularly visiting their homes and discreetly relieving distress caused by death or other family tragedy. George V even helped the son of an estate worker with his mathematics homework one evening. However the boy refused a second offer a few weeks later. 'Oh, I see you have progressed beyond me, is that it?' the King asked. 'No sir,' replied the lad, 'but you got it wrong last time.'

The short-lived reign of Edward VIII was long enough for many on the estate. His cost-cutting exercises caused consternation, especially as

the same men who loaded champagne into his Buick for Mrs Simpson had had their beer money stopped. The number of game birds was drastically reduced while George V's flax-growing experiment at Flitcham was scrapped. It was all too much for the Sandringham agent, Edmund Beck, who resigned his post.

When George VI became King he introduced reforms in a gradual, conciliatory way that has been the hallmark of the last fifty years. In recent times the Duke of Edinburgh has been the innovator, scientifically developing the 2,000 acres of woodland and reclaiming 700 acres of coastline for farmland.

The lifestyle at Sandringham is vigorously rural and the Queen is a familiar figure along the lanes with her black Labrador gun dogs at her heel and a green Land Rover containing her Scotland Yard bodyguards following at a discreet distance.

It is here that her childhood dream of being an anonymous country woman surrounded by

BELOW: *The royal dogs are always buried at Sandringham. There is no proper graveyard but they are placed in pretty spots.* RIGHT: *Hyacinths and roses provide a homely counterpoint to the coats of armour and tapestries inside the House.*

dogs and horses is realized. 'I hope you don't mind my saying,' said the American tourist to the lady in a headscarf in a Norfolk teashop, 'but you do look awfully like the Queen.'

'How very reassuring,' smiled the Queen as she and her lady-in-waiting left the shop. As an active countrywoman, she and the other royal ladies take part in the work of the local Women's Institute, the Queen regularly giving talks while Princess Margaret pours the tea. Her last was about the exploits of 'her boys' from the royal yacht *Britannia* when they rescued refugees from fighting in Aden. One year the Queen Mother and her daughters were photographed walking out of a meeting with milk churns balanced on top of their heads.

Sandingham provides the Queen with a welcome break from the affairs of State. In his *Diaries* the former Labour Cabinet Minister, Richard Crossman, observed:

They all love this place. It has become a family hideout, where they feel like human beings. It would be nice if one could arrange for the Queen to commute from Sandringham and use Buckingham Palace as an office.

Edward VII leads his fabled racehorse, Persimmon, winner of the 1896 Derby. The king always enjoyed gambling on the outcome of a race.

Like the Queen herself, Sandringham is a blend of the homely and the grand. Goya portraits from the Royal Collection hang above a clothes horse bedecked with Christmas cards, and the Queen will feed her corgis breadsticks under the table at a black tie dinner. 'It is a very comfortable place, very welcoming,' recalls one guest, who was surprised by the sight of a nodding china corgi top placed on top of the grand piano in the Great Saloon. 'It has the smell of fresh flowers and polish.'

They might also have added that Sandringham is suffused with the tradition of generations of royal horse owners. From the statue of Persimmon, Edward VII's legendary Derby winner, to the horse brasses in the hallway, Sandringham is the home of the sport of kings.

As Prince of Wales, Edward VII was absorbed in racing. One critic noted that he attended twenty-eight race meetings in 1890, nearly three times as many days as he attended in the House of Lords. He enjoyed the glamorous camaraderie of the racing set and the excitement of a race, regularly placing heavy bets on the outcome. Shortly after his return from India in 1875 the Prince, encouraged by Lord Marcus Beresford who later became manager of the royal stud, began to build up his own stable that was to be the foundation of the royal family's continued fascination for the sport.

His most notable successes were three Derby winners – Persimmon in 1896, Diamond Jubilee in 1900 and Minoru in 1909 – together with Ambush II who won the Grand National in 1900. In that year he headed the list of winning owners with £29,586 ($143,000).

Edward VII's love of the sport brought him widespread popularity although his lucky streak seemed to desert him throughout the middle years of his reign when he scarcely had a winner. However, over the years he had established himself as perhaps the most successful owner breeder in Britain, earning £500,000 ($2.42 million) in fees from stallions, stakes and sales.

Like his father, George V enjoyed the carnival atmosphere of a big race day but he was an unlucky owner, winning his first classic race, the One Thousand Guineas, at the twenty-fourth attempt. Like most gamblers, he rarely came out on top during the course of a season. In his diary following the defeat of Scuttle in the Oaks of 1928 he noted, 'We returned home wiser but certainly poorer.' The King also

Royal Ascot has always been a racing and social event. The 1908 meeting was no exception.

endured the distressing episode at the 1913 Derby when a suffragette threw herself under the King's horse, Anmer, as the field swept round Tattenham Corner. 'A most regrettable, scandalous proceeding,' he recalled. By 1935 he had no horse in training of any merit and, as ill-fortune dogged the royal stables, the prospect of closing the Sandringham studs loomed. Ironically, the year of the Abdication brought a string of successes which convinced George VI that he should continue.

Always a keen and competent horsewoman, the Queen developed a passionate interest in racing as a teenager – an enthusiasm nurtured by her mother who today has a bookie's blower installed at Clarence House, and by George VI's racing manager, Captain Charles Moore. Her enthusiasm was well known and when she married her wedding gifts included prints of Newmarket racing scenes, several pairs of binoculars, a saddle from the Saddlers'

Company and, best of all, a filly from the Aga Khan. She called her Astrakhan who went on to fulfil her early promise by winning at the now defunct Hurst Park in 1949.

Later that year Lord Mildmay of Flete, the legendary amateur rider, persuaded the Queen and the Princess Elizabeth to buy Monaveen, a sturdy Irish steeplechaser. It won several races over the sticks before tragedy struck. In 1950 he broke his leg at the Hurst Park water jump and, to the dismay of the Princess, had to be put down. Her enthusiasm for National Hunt racing never really recovered and since then she has left the 'sticks' to her mother, while she dedicated herself to the Flat.

In the summer of the Coronation in 1953, as the whole country buzzed with excitement, the Queen's thoughts were with her horses. During the frantic days before the ceremony at Westminster Abbey, the Queen scored her first major success as an owner when Aureole won the Derby Trial at Lingfield and was then strongly tipped to take the blue ribbon event. The Coronation was to take place on the

Tuesday; the Derby on the Saturday. On Monday, one of the Queen's ladies-in-waiting said to her, 'You look so calm, ma'am, but you must be anxious.'

'I am,' nodded the Queen, 'but all the same I think Aureole will win.' The Queen's favourite was pipped at the post but went on to win the immensely valuable King George VI and Queen Elizabeth Stakes at Royal Ascot the following year. For over a decade Aureole – nicknamed 'Ginger' by the Queen – was serving some forty mares a year at 1,000 ($2,800) guineas a time, earning his mistress £40,000 ($112,000) a year in stud fees. In those early days the Queen clearly had a winning touch, amassing over £40,000 ($112,000) in prizes in 1954, with her horses winning nineteen races. Perhaps it was the lucky china horse that young Prince Charles bought her at Badminton horse trials which brought such good fortune. Certainly the Queen set much store by the token. On the opening day of Royal Ascot in 1957 – a year where she was the leading owner with thirty wins – she realized that she had left the china horse behind at Windsor Castle and requested her equerry to fetch it. In that season she received prize money of more than £62,000 ($173,000).

However, during the 1960s the royal colours of purple and gold were rarely seen in the winners' enclosure. In 1968 she had such a poor year that she cut back her horses in training from twenty-eight to fourteen. Two years later Lord Porchester, now Earl Carnarvon, became (and remains) her racing manager and her fortunes changed. In 1970, with only six horses in training, she won fifteen races and £25,755 ($61,800).

While Prince Charles once admitted that every time he bet on his mother's horses it ended in disaster, by 1979 her overall return in racing of £1 million had handsomely out-stripped that of her great-grandfather, Edward VII. The Queen is no idle bystander and when she visits the royal stud is quite prepared to fetch and carry pails of feed and water. As her racing manager observes, 'She is keenly interested in every aspect of her string and is regarded as being one of the world's experts.'

Appropriately enough the Queen's Silver Jubilee in 1977 saw the Queen topping the British winning breeders list. 'If if were not for my Archbishop of Canterbury,' she observed, 'I should be off in my plane to Longchamps every

Sunday.' Scarcely surprising since during the 1970s the Queen won the French Oaks and numerous other races across the Channel.

However, the Derby has eluded her: to win it remains an ambition close to her heart. Lord Carnarvon is hopeful, 'In terms of the financing of the racing and breeding operation we are very much in profit and what's more I think we have every chance of breeding a Derby winner for the Queen.' He is quick to emphasize that the Queen's stables are run entirely independently of the Civil List and must show an independent profit.

The Queen has proved a shrewd commercial judge in the racing business. In 1982 she invested over £800,000 ($1.85 million) in stables run by Major Dick Hern, buying the property from its owners, Lord Weinstock and Lord Sobell. Lord Carnarvon explains, 'Our aim is to make the risky game of breeding as much of a self-financing exercise as possible. The Queen has added a sound investment in bricks and mortar to her horses.'

This expenditure – the stables are now worth £1,500,000 ($2.55 million) – was financed by the sale of one of the Queen's most presti-gious fillies, Height of Fashion, to Sheik Maktoum for a reported £1,250,000 ($2.9 million).

While the 1980s have proved to be lean years for prize money, the Queen has, over the decades, made a considerable investment in racehorses and stud facilities. Unlike her other investments, the price of the Queen's race-horses are not inflated by the royal owner, merely their ability to win races. In 1989 a London firm of bloodstock valuers discreetly assessed the Queen's stable for this book. Their valuation is conservative as, in terms of breed-ing and racing performance, the Queen's stable is currently not outstanding. This is inspite of owning racehorses sired by such stallions as Mill Reef, Shirley Heights and Mummy's Pet. Obviously a run of wins during a future season would dramatically increase their value.

The Queen has thirty-one horses in training, worth around £750,000 ($1,275,000), twenty-three brood mares and their foals, worth about £1,750,000 ($2,975,000) and fifteen yearlings with a market value of £225,000 ($382,500). Her nineteen stallion shares – Bustino and Shirley Heights take the majority – are estim-ated to be worth £500,000 ($850,000). In total the Queen's investment in pedigree horseflesh

*The Queen meets the newly-knighted jockey Gordon
Richards before the Coronation Derby.*

is between £3,000,000 ($4.5 million) and
£3,500,000 ($5.95 million). This of course
excludes her considerable investment in the

royal studs at Sandringham and West Ilsley,
Berkshire.

With such an enormous investment at stake
well may the Queen hope that the Prince of
Wales soon takes an interest in racing. Like
Prince Philip, Prince Charles only stays at

145

The Queen has one supreme racing ambition – to breed a Derby winner.

Royal Ascot for a couple of races each afternoon before driving off to nearby Smith's Lawn to play polo.

This indifference to racing probably worries the Queen who takes her horse racing very seriously, using every technological advance to the full. Just as Edward VII introduced one of the first ticker tape machines to Marlborough House, so the Queen has a £25,000 ($57,000) computer, a gift from President Reagan, installed at Lord Carnarvon's Highclere stud in Wiltshire. It has a direct link to bloodstock centres in Kentucky, giving the Queen a full breakdown of the lineage of any horse in the world within seconds.

The high tech world of racing thoroughbreds epitomizes the briskly businesslike way she and the Duke of Edinburgh have managed the private royal estates of Balmoral, Sandringham and West Ilsley. Here the Sovereign and her family are fully involved and have complete control over their investments. This approach differs with her other significant estate, the Duchy of Lancaster, which comprises ancient lands devolved to her by right as Sovereign. Here she is effectively a custodian as opposed to the owner and this governs her attitude to these holdings. Quite properly she conforms to centuries-old precedent and practise, allowing agents to make the major commercial decisions.

Traditionally, the Duchy of Lancaster (in 1988 it yielded a tax-free income of around

£2,270,000 ([$3,859,000]), finances the Privy Purse, which offsets the cost of private expenditure that is not otherwise covered by the Civil List but arises from the Queen's duties as Head of State. Duchy profits go towards her extensive wardrobe of clothes, the maintenance of Balmoral and Sandringham, her wide range of charitable contributions and pensions for her employees who are not otherwise provided for.

This estate of 52,000 acres of farm and moorland was created in 1265 when King Henry III seized the lands of the defeated rebel baron, Simon de Montfort, and gave them to the King's youngest son, Edmund, as an inheritance. The office of Chancellor of the Duchy of Lancaster was created in 1363 to oversee the management of the estates and today survives as a political appointment.

While the Queen tries to inspect some of the farms and regularly invites tenants to her garden parties at Buckingham Palace, there is little feeling here of the Queen knowing locals by name and becoming involved in the community. She has a very proper, rather distant relationship with the Duchy, far more formal than with her privately owned properties.

The Duchy itself is divided into four regions known as 'surveys', which are principally found in Yorkshire, Lancashire, Cheshire and Staffordshire. However, the best known-property lies on the south side of the Strand in London. This is the Queen's Chapel of the Savoy which today acts as the chapel of the Royal Victorian Order, the decoration bestowed personally by the Queen on her family and staff.

If the Queen were ever to sell this 700-year-old estate it would have a market value of around £55 million ($93.5 million), a conservative valuation bearing in mind the long leases held by tenants and the agricultural nature of the land.

Most confusion regarding the Queen's private wealth surrounds the Crown Estate. These lands, once owned by the monarch but surrendered by George III in return for the Civil List, occupy a curious constitutional position. It is a tradition that they are surrendered afresh to Parliament by the Sovereign at the beginning of each reign as part of the arrangements for the Civil List provision. Technically, they are neither fully owned by the Government nor the private property of the reigning monarch. This is something of a legal fiction that has little

The Queen and her racing manager, Earl Carnarvon, cast keen eyes over a thoroughbred during a private visit to Kentucky.

basis in reality – rather like the Queen's continuing right to declare war at will. The Crown Estate Commissioners admitted as much to the 1971 Parliamentary Inquiry into the Civil List where they conceded that the land was effectively public property.

It might be argued that the monarch has done badly out of the exchange of Crown Lands for the Civil List as the Crown Estate revenue, roughly £50 million ($85 million) a year, far outweighs the Civil List allowance of around £6 million. However, the Crown Estate was originally passed to Parliament in return for relieving the monarch of the burden of providing for the entire cost of the nation's civil administration. If this cost is added in then monarchy is seen to have done rather well out of the transaction.

Yet the myth continues that the Crown Estate, valued in 1988 at £1.2 billion ($2.04 billion) and taking in Trafalgar Square, the Strand and much of Regent Street, belongs to the Queen. Even Prince Charles argued as much in an interview with Penny Junor:

The royal family must have money. If they have to look to the State for everything, they become nothing more than puppets, and prisoners in their own countries. That's what's happened to the Japanese royal family. They can't even go on holiday without asking Parliament.

That would be an intolerable situation; but I think it might be a good idea if the royal family stopped receiving money from the Civil List and lived instead on the income from the Crown Estate. That seems sensible to me, although I suspect I might get some opposition.

Prince Charles' own estate, the Duchy of Cornwall, is relatively straightforward. The Duchy was created in 1337 by King Edward III who gave a large parcel of land in Cornwall to his son, Edward, the Black Prince, for his maintenance.

Prince Charles is the twenty-fifth Duke of Cornwall, becoming Duke when the Queen ascended the throne in 1952 but not receiving the revenues from the 126,000-acre estate until he was eighteen. When he took over the Duchy in 1969 he inherited an estate that had been without ducal supervision since the Abdication of Edward VIII in 1936 and was therefore in need of firm control from the top.

It was old-fashioned and inefficient, offering little encouragement to the tenants to improve their farming practices. Since his marriage, the Prince has reformed the Duchy, increasing rents, sweeping away outdated restrictions, and improving property. He has also spent several weeks on various farms in Devon and Cornwall, learning at first hand about the concerns of his tenants.

While the Prince owns much of the rugged moorland of Dartmoor, including Dartmoor Prison, it is his 41 acres of property in Kennington, south London, which are the most valuable. In 1987 he sold Newquay House for £1.2 million ($2.04 million), while two other London sales raised £1.9 million ($3.23 million). This valuable land, which incorporates the Oval Test cricket ground, makes his Duchy estate worth around £250 million ($425 million).

The Prince is technically exempt from tax but he pays 25 per cent of his £1.9 million ($3.123 million) annual income as a voluntary contribution to the Consolidated Fund, the equivalent of a State kitty. Before he married he donated 50 per cent.

When the Prince becomes King, it will be Prince William who will inherit the Duchy of Cornwall estate together with his country home of Highgrove in Gloucestershire, which the Duchy bought for £800,000 ($1.85 million) in 1980. The nine-bedroomed house and surrounding 757 acres of organic farmland are now valued at £3.2 million ($5.44 million) at today's prices.

Like Edward VIII who as Prince of Wales had an uneconomic 4,000-acre farm in Alberta, Canada, Prince Charles does have property abroad. However, his acceptance of a £360,000 ($835,000) holiday home in Palm Beach as a wedding gift created a political storm. Numerous MPs, including Conservative MP Teddy Taylor, accused property developer Bill Ylvisaker of cashing in on the royal connection while lurid headlines told of 'Royal home in drug belt'. Charles, who plays polo a couple of times a year at the West Palm Beach ground, has used the four-bedroomed home as his base during brief visits.

RIGHT: *While the Queen is the owner of a decent-sized racing stable she still helps out, fetching pails of water and feed for her horses whilst rewarding them with hardboiled mints.*

ABOVE: *Princess Margaret's hideaway home, Les Jolies Eaux, on Mustique.*

There was no such protest when Colin Tennant, now Lord Glenconner, gave Princess Margaret a plot of land on his island of Mustique in the Caribbean. He had asked the Princess if she would like something wrapped in a box from Asprey's or the clifftop site on his island. She chose the land, Tennant agreeing to build her the cream-painted plantation house she called *Les Jolies Eaux*. In her drawing-room she has a large portrait of the Queen, 'It's so that people from abroad can see it's an English house,' she tells visitors. On the nearby island of Antigua Princess Michael of Kent accepted a plot of land from her friend, Peter de Savary, which has since been sold.

The Queen has remained conservatively British in her landholdings, although myth maintains that the Queen is, to quote *Fortune*, the American financial magazine, 'reputedly one of the largest landowners in Manhattan' with 'large holdings in Germany and France'.

The origin of this story was a headline in the now defunct *New York Mirror* of June 1963 which posed the question: 'Does Queen own Old Pornopolis?', implying that she was the hidden landlady in New York's notorious blue light district around 42nd Street. This inaccurate story has gained currency so that today it is accepted as fact.

The story of land owned in Europe derives from Queen Victoria's ownership of land in Coburg and a villa in Baden. They have long been sold. Does the Queen have any property overseas? The written answer from Buckingham Palace is a straight denial. Her one overseas possession, Sagana Lodge in Kenya, which was given as a wedding present, was returned to the Government of Kenya on Independence in 1963.

The Queen may be the most widely travelled monarch in history, but her roots are firmly bedded within her kingdom. Her love of horses follows in the traditions of her forefathers and her occasional holidays abroad are invariably to judge the horseflesh on offer from the blue grass state of Kentucky. Her energies and those of the Duke of Edinburgh and the Prince of Wales have been channelled into improving and extending their British landholdings. Their wise husbandry and shrewd horse sense has meant that their private royal kingdom is greater than at any time in the last 200 years.

OPPOSITE: *The Queen and Queen Mother discuss the form guide before the start of a Derby.*

5
A Goodly Heritage

A certain stern dignity surrounds the royal perambulator. Its glossy black and maroon paintwork is highly polished, a gold royal crest on the side signifying the station of the infant lying snugly within the sturdy coach-built frame.

The royal perambulator lasts far more than a lifetime. The Princess of Wales took Prince William for walks around Kensington Gardens using the same pram which nanny Alla Knight had for baby Princess Elizabeth and her successor, Mabel Anderson, for Prince Charles. No doubt Prince William's children will have their first memories of the world outside formed in precisely the same way as their great-grandmother.

The only alterations to familiar routine have been the incursions of security. Until quite recently it was felt sufficient to secrete a whistle under the covers for Nanny to use in case of danger to her royal charge. Now a Scotland Yard detective complete with walkie talkie and hand gun goes too.

In the royal nursery Princes William and Harry play with many of the toys their father enjoyed. Like Prince Charles, Prince Harry

BELOW: *The sturdy royal perambulator symbolizes continuity and tradition within the Windsor dynasty. Here George V leads Princess Elizabeth and her nanny at a Balmoral fête while* RIGHT: *the young Duke of Gloucester casts a watchful gaze over his young cousin, Prince Charles.*

learned to walk holding on to a tatty pushalong donkey, while Prince William plays with the same Hans Christian Andersen style wooden soldiers at Windsor Castle that the Queen's children used for their own make believe military manoeuvres. Princess Anne learned to ride on the same rocking horse that Princesses Elizabeth and Margaret played with at 145 Piccadilly in London.

While Prince William enjoys racing around the Highgrove estate in a fully working miniature Jaguar he was given by the Midlands car factory, his father's own turquoise pedal car, registration number PC 1, is on display outside

153

the private garden entrance at Buckingham Palace.

The royal family are willing hostages to their heritage, from the Honiton lace christening robe used for every new royal arrival since Queen Victoria's day to the annual Court round

ABOVE: *A scale model of Prince Charles' Aston Martin sports car made especially for Prince William.* BELOW: *The young Prince Charles in his own runabout, now at Buckingham Palace.*

of Sandringham, Windsor Castle and Balmoral. 'Is it how my father did it? Then I will do it,' was the Queen's familiar refrain during the early days of her reign.

The uniforms and clothes of George VI and those of his father, George V, are still carefully preserved under polythene covers at Buckingham Palace and occasionally dusted down by a royal valet. Indeed, there were gasps of dismay within the family when the Princess of Wales blithely admitted that she gives clothes from her own over-extended wardrobe to her friends and family. At one wedding she discovered to her amusement that several of the guests were wearing her cast offs.

Innovation is regarded as a regrettable necessity and delayed wherever possible. For example, when the Queen arranged to have new curtains in the yellow drawing room at Buckingham Palace she had to cancel the appointment because she was sitting for the portrait painter, Michael Noakes. She promised to look at the samples and the designer left behind his swatch of fabric samples. It was four years before the Queen eventually found the time and inclination to make a decision.

The Windsor heritage of paintings, photographs, *objets d'art*, furniture, gold plate and

The royal christening robe of Honiton lace has been used by the royal family since 1841, most recently for the christening of Princess Beatrice.

silverware are among the finest and most extensive privately administered collections in the world. Successive royal generations have added to an inheritance they have gradually shared with the nation and Commonwealth. The Queen and the Duke of Edinburgh have been active in bringing the Royal Collections to a wider public by rebuilding the bombed-out chapel at Buckingham Palace for the Queen's Gallery, which since 1962 has given people a chance to view at first hand the royal treasures. One day perhaps even Buckingham Palace – a royal home for which few members of the family have any affection – may become a national museum like the Louvre in Paris where the public may appreciate the full sweep and grandeur of the Royal Collections.

Like previous sovereigns, the Queen sees herself as guardian to a fabulous national treasure that reflects the cultural life of Britain and the Empire. Royal generosity has formed the basis for collections in several major galleries and museums. William IV gave two enormous libraries, including rare religious manuscripts, to the British Museum while Queen Victoria donated Renaissance masterpieces to the National Gallery. This relationship, the giving and receiving, is at the heart of our understanding of monarchy. Just as the royal family receive tribute, so they pay tribute to the nation, their own munificence enriching the national life.

Caretakers of a profound heritage, they are also avid collectors in their own right, their private interests giving an insight into their characters. While the Queen Mother made numerous additions to the national heritage of paintings, she has also assembled a small but distinguished collection of French Impressionist and modern English paintings in her own right. Unlike other collectors, the royal family are not attracted to objects as investments but for the pleasure they bring. Prince Charles saves Eskimo carvings, George VI collected Fabergé cigarette cases, Princess Margaret has a hexagonal case designed by Lord Snowdon for her seashell collection, while the Duchess of York has followed in the footsteps of the Queen Mother and collects paintings which delight or amuse her.

Clearly, the task of making a distinction between the 'inalienable' collections which are held in trust and those which are privately owned by the Queen and the rest of the family is difficult. Lord Cobbold gave the following ruling in his evidence to the Parliamentary Select Committee on the Civil List in 1971: 'The Royal Collection is regarded as covering all pictures and works of art purchased or acquired by all Sovereigns *up to the death of Queen Victoria* (my italics) and also certain property acquired by Sovereigns and their Consorts since the death of Queen Victoria, which was specially allocated to the Royal Collection. This of course covers the vast bulk of the contents of the Royal Palaces. The Royal Collection is regarded as passing in right of the Crown from Sovereign to Sovereign and, therefore, inalienable by the occupant of the throne.'

He made the additional points that some minor items are occasionally sold to raise funds to purchase more relevant works for the Collection and that duplicate material is given away as presents to the Commonwealth.

However, this quite properly leaves out the jewels and memorabilia defined as family heirlooms. This ruling also gives the present Queen wide discretion to choose works of art inherited from reigns since 1901 to place into the Royal Collection.

There is an important legal precedent which casts light on the distinction between the Royal and private collections. In 1950 the case of Leaf *v.* International Galleries produced the ruling that the works of well-known artists such as Constable and Canaletto may not be disposed of under normal commercial rules and sold at will. It follows that contemporary paintings held by members of the royal family may be considered to be privately owned whilst their Old Masters would be defined as coming under the orbit of 'national heritage.'

The difficulties over when a private royal possession becomes part of the national heritage was illustrated in the legal wrangling over George V's stamp collection, and underlined with Queen Mary's Doll's House. Although she left it in her will to the Queen Mother, it is now in the Queen's possession and is part of the Royal Collection. Its sale would be considered a loss to the national heritage.

While the Royal Collections are so extensive that whole suits of armour have been mislaid for decades, the private royal possessions have a scale which also spans the centuries.

Whenever the royal family are asked to contribute to charity auctions, their donations hint at the range of their personal possessions. When the Queen gave a George III mustard pot and spoon for auction in aid of the Chichester Cathedral Trust it raised £3,600 ($8,350) while a rosewood and brass trinket box, once belonging to George IV and donated by the Queen Mother, raised £440 ($1,020). For another event the Queen Mother gave a silver gilt porringer in the Charles II style, while the Queen's donation of a pink Fabergé elephant, barely an inch high, raised £7,250 ($16,820) for the Duke of Edinburgh's Award scheme.

If and when royal pieces are sold at auction they naturally attract a considerable premium. In 1982 six items of furniture from Holyrood House in Scotland raised £16,250 ($37,700), three times the anticipated amount. One Australian flew to Glasgow to bid in the auction at Christie's in Glasgow. The sale was held to help pay for the upkeep of the ancient royal seat. Prior to the auction a Buckingham Palace official was quoted as saying that all the furniture was the Queen's own property.

OPPOSITE: *Queen Mary's famous doll's house. Craftsmen and artists throughout the Empire made tiny contributions.*

BATHROOM   LINEN ROOM   HOUSEKEEPER'S ROOM

Seventy-five leather-bound volumes at Windsor Castle alone are required to list the furniture and other works of art contained within its thick walls, while Queen Mary's personal collection runs to three stout books.

An indication of the magnitude and value of the royal family's private collection was demonstrated by the world's biggest sale of *objets d'art* at Mentmore Towers, the palatial home of the Earl of Rosebery, in 1977. The 2,702 lots sold for £6,389,933 ($14,696,845) – around £15 million ($25.5 million) at today's prices – in several days of frenzied bidding where the final total was twice Sotheby's estimate.

If the private possessions of the House of Windsor ever went under the hammer the historical provenance of the collection would add considerably to its value in much the same way as the Duchess of Windsor's jewels were inflated by a factor of ten because of their regal associations. At the same time the sale of the Earl of Rosebery's goods and chattels is a useful indicator of the kind of sums even a middle-ranking aristocrat can command.

The royal family occupy or own enough space to accommodate a decent sized-country town – Buckingham Palace even has its own post office – yet still their collections crowd every corner. A valuation of £260 million ($442 million) on their innumerable possessions is but a cautious estimate on this unique hoard of items which range from Regency furniture, Oriental jade,

Chelsea porcelain, silver snuff boxes and diamond encrusted fans. It is a heritage which surrounds every royal child as the Duke of York recalled when he reflected on his childhood: 'I always took care of the precious objects when they weren't in the way. We used to play football along the passageway and every now and again a pane of glass got broken but I don't think we ever broke a piece of Meissen or anything like that.'

ABOVE: *A herd of Fabergé elephants. The largest, which works by clockwork, was given to George V on Christmas Day in 1929.* BELOW: *Many carved Fabergé animals are kept in a secret vault.*

He did however come close to breaking a Fabergé Easter egg – worth £1 million ($1.7 million) – during a photographic session. He knocked it off the shelf but managed to catch it before the exquisite piece, which hides a delicate angel, plummeted to the floor.

Queen Alexandra, as Princess of Wales, accepted the first piece of Fabergé when she attended the wedding of the young Emperor and Empress of Russia at the Anitchkoff Palace in 1894. Her sister Minnie, the Dowager Empress Marie Feodorovna, marked the occasion by giving the Princess a beautiful crystal flower in a gold pot, made by Carl Fabergé, with a great diamond at its centre.

At the time these gifts were regarded as delightful, whimsical trinkets which the sisters showered on each other for birthdays, Christmas and other special occasions. In 1907 Edward VII sent to St Petersburg for Fabergé modellers and asked them to make miniatures of all the animals on the Sandringham farm. Working quickly and nimbly they made models in semi-precious stones of everything from their huge shire horses, the King's dog Caesar – who had his own footman – to Queen Alexandra's pet Pekinese. They were assembled in the dairy and naturally when the Queen saw them she was enraptured.

The mosaic egg containing profiles of the Russian Imperial children who were later murdered.

Queen Mary added to the already impressive Palace collection, taking advantage of the Bolsheviks' desire to sell off their heritage and bring in hard currency to aid Russia's desperate economy. On 26th November, 1927, for example, she walked into Wartski's show-room in London's West End and bought the miniature grand piano for £75 ($364) and on 12th October, 1929, she acquired the Colonnade Egg for just £500 ($2,450).

Her most notable purchases were two Imperial eggs, one poignantly containing a cameo upon which are carved portraits of the five Imperial children, which were carried out only five years before their murder in 1918. Her love of Fabergé was passed on to her son, George VI, who made a fine collection of cigarette cases which he used constantly.

For a small investment the royal family have acquired an imcomparable collection which is today worth at least £13 million ($22.1 million), according to an expert assessment by Laurence Krashes who also valued the royal jewellery for this book. The eggs alone now go at auction for a fraction under £2 million ($3.4 million) while the flower arrangements, which so enchanted Queen Alexandra, sell for £30,000 ($51,000). More the pity then, that so many of these eclectic examples of elegant Edwardian caprice have ended their days under a plastic sheet in the underground vault at Buckingham Palace.

Nonetheless, each new generation wants to shape the royal House in the image of its own times. While seeking to preserve the past they also make their own indelible stamp on the present. So Edward VII cleared away the detritus from his mother's long reign — she was in the habit of taking enormous numbers of pictures, photographs and treasured possessions whenever she travelled — and in her turn, Queen Mary regally springcleaned the clouds of sentimental relics left by Queen Alexandra. 'Such a bewildering lot of things and pictures . . . all the rooms are more airey now and less full of those odds and ends which beloved Mama would poke into every corner of the house which was such a pity,' she wrote after taking up residence in Sandringham. Her maid may have dissented — she regularly cleared ninety curios from Queen Mary's dressing table before she polished.

Queen Mary, the great royal collector, with choice pieces of Chinese hardstone carvings.

Queen Mary was the most avid collector. If she saw something she wanted she took steps to acquire it, employing every strategem in her considerable armoury.

George V's biographer, Kenneth Rose, described her technique splendidly:

Visiting the homes of friends, acquaintances and strangers, sometimes self invited, she would stand in front of a covetable object and pronounce in measured tones: "I am caressing it with my eyes." If that evoked no impulsive gesture of generosity, the Queen would resume her tour. But on taking her leave, she would pause on the doorstep and ask: "May I go back and say goodbye to that dear little cabinet?" Should even that touching appeal fail to melt the granite heart of her host, her letter of thanks might include a request to buy the piece. Few could resist that final assault.

When she had to pay for an item the Queen was quite prepared to haggle, the negotiations taking place through her lady-in-waiting. While furniture, plate and china absorbed her, the Queen's obsession with miniatures was her Achilles' heal. Glass cases at Sandringham and Marlborough House bore testimony to her love of tiny golden tea sets, minute chairs in mother of pearl and of course her pride and joy, the famous Doll's House.

The relish with which she set about redecorating Sandringham and Buckingham Palace was matched by the zeal she displayed in organizing the Crown Collections. There is hardly a piece of furniture or work of art in the remotest room or back corridor which does not have a label in Queen Mary's fluid script describing its subject or origin.

While she was a diligent and thorough collator, Queen Mary was no innovator or abiter of taste. Yet her ceaseless detective work provided her with an absorbing hobby and greatly enriched both the Royal Collections and the former royal residences of Holyrood House and the Brighton Pavilion which underwent restoration during her lifetime.

She was a familiar figure in the antique shops of King's Lynn and Kensington as she poked around in corners looking for 'tempting things'. As one dealer recalled affectionately:

She loved "spotting" things in odd corners — wise men made sure the things were there to be spotted when they knew she was coming. It was a game well understood by both sides, a charming ritual.

Her obsession with 'her one great hobby' occasionally exasperated George V. 'There you go again, May – always furniture, furniture, furniture,' he cried when he overheard her asking dinner guests about new pieces. However it didn't stop him from talking about his own passion of stamp collecting.

During her long life Queen Mary acquired scores of lacquered boxes, fine Chinese jade, Battersea and Canton enamels, and tiny watercolours. Her collection was so great that when she rewrote her will in favour of the present Queen following George VI's death she spent two months sorting through what she called 'my interesting things'.

Her phenomenal memory was legendary. When her brother, the Marquis of Cambridge, died in 1927 she went through the long list of objects he left noting by the side of each one who had acquired it. The dread letter 'Z' appeared next to those heirlooms which had gone missing. This meant there would be an extended inquest to discover its whereabouts.

While the regal eye for detail is unremitting – Prince Philip and Prince Charles can spot a misplaced military decoration from fifty paces – subsequent royal generations have not been as consumed with collecting mania as Queen Mary. The Queen Mother has shown a greater discernment, and not a little wit and adventure in her enthusiastic patronage of modern British and European artists. In the last fifty years the Royal Collection of paintings, both personal and Crown, has undergone its most vigorous revival in 120 years.

Augustus John's portrait of Bernard Shaw with his eyes shut – cheekily entitled *When Homer Nods* – shows the sense of humour the Queen Mother brought to bear when buying pictures. She even agreed to pose for the taciturn artist at Buckingham Palace during the war. However, the drawing-rooms were so cold that she abandoned the project because she became frozen during the sittings.

Her affection for Italy and France where she spends many holidays has influenced her choice of paintings. Impressionist works by Monet and Sisley decorate her homes in Scotland and England and her enjoyment of modern artists ensured that she was pleased to accept a bequest from her friend, Viscountess Waverley, of works by Berthe Morisot who was of the Manet school. Walter Sickert and Matthew Smith together with L. S. Lowry,

The collection of Meissen at Glamis Castle in Scotland inspired the Queen Mother's life-long love of porcelain.

Duncan Grant and Paul Nash are other modern artists who have caught her eye.

Pictures by the Herrings and Wilson Steer represent her traditional taste while a stark abstract by Alan Davie shows her sense of enterprise, a characteristic displayed when she asked the candidly controversial artist Graham Sutherland to paint her. His severe study of Winston Churchill so infuriated Lady Churchill that she destroyed it.

Prince Charles sketching on the banks of the river Dee. He prefers watercolours to oils.

The Queen Mother's interest marked a watershed in the fortunes of the Royal Collection. After the war the exhibition, The King's Pictures, at the Royal Academy attracted 366,000 visitors. Queen Mary was suitably impressed, recording in her diary, 'Met Bertie and all the family there, many artists etc – The pictures looked lovely and were well hung by Mr Blunt* and the Committee, all the rooms were filled – A most enjoyable afternoon.'

While Queen Mary found it difficult to communicate her enthusiasms to her children, the Queen Mother's love of the arts has been passed on to the Queen and her grandson, the Prince of Wales. One of Princess Elizabeth's wedding gifts was a Paul Nash painting and she has also taken up her mother's interest in porcelain and china. The Queen Mother has a fine assembly of Chelsea porcelain, among which are many plates made by the famous eighteenth-century manufacturer, Hans Sloane.

The Queen has encouraged Scottish and Commonwealth artists, in particular Australian painters like Russell Drysdale and Rex Batterbee. In her private collection on display in her apartments at Buckingham Palace are works by popular, conventional artists like Norman Wilkinson, James Gunn, Gerald Kelly and Winston Churchill for whom she formed a great affection. She commissioned a bust of Churchill which now stands in the Queen's Guard Chamber at Windsor Castle.

Visiting friends may also see a prized study of a child, *The Daisy Chain*, by the now fashionable Edwardian watercolourist, Rose Barton. As Princess of Wales, Queen Mary favoured her with commissions for family Christmas presents. Recently a group of her impressionistic paintings of London at the turn of the century sold for £120,000 ($204,000), emphasizing the value that lies in even obscure corners of the private Royal Collections.

The Duke of Edinburgh, a former Naval officer, has shown a keen interest in seascapes and took the highly respected seascape artist Edward Seago on his famous circumnavigation of the globe on the royal yacht *Britannia* in 1957. His children know of his interest and frequently add to his collection of nautical views – the Princess Royal paid £175 ($298) for a view of *Britannia* at anchor in Venice for his sixty-fifth birthday.

* Later Sir Anthony Blunt, Surveyor of the Queen's Pictures, and unmasked as a Soviet spy.

He admires, too, the irreverent caricatures by Felix Topolski and has walls covered in framed newspaper cartoons. The Duke and Duchess of York have formed a similar attachment.

Like his father, Prince Charles is a not inconsiderable artist in his own right. While the Duke is attracted to bold oils, the Prince prefers the subtler medium of watercolours. He has formed friendships with the watercolourist John Ward and the young oil painter Martin Yeoman. Both have been invited on board the royal yacht during official visits to give the Prince tuition. Ward's charming study of the Princess of Wales in her wedding dress hangs on the staircase at Kensington Palace.

His efforts on behalf of the National Gallery to secure the celebrated Holbein portrait of Henry VIII from the collection of Baron Thyssen demonstrates that the Queen's commitment to the world of fine art will be in safe hands with the future King. It emphasizes, too, the collaboration between the royal family and the nation in augmenting Britain's heritage.

The Queen's additions to the Royal Collection have been justly celebrated as the finest since the death of the Prince Consort. *The Burlington Magazine's* editorial of August 1962 underlined the Sovereign's contribution: 'She has bought a number of interesting Royal portraits and some contemporary English paintings which will one day take their place in the Royal Collection. She has stimulated and initiated the cleaning and the rearrangement of her

The royal yacht Britannia *in Venice.*

pictures, particularly at Windsor. Thanks to the Queen's enthusiasm . . . the Royal Collection is now very much alive.'

This magnificent collection of 5,000 important paintings and 30,000 drawings* by masters like Leonardo da Vinci, Michelangelo, Raphael, Dürer, Holbein, Bernini and Canaletto is a 'lone and proud survivor' of the days when the Bourbons, the Valois, the Habsburgs and numerous other royal families inspired and sponsored the arts. As the former Surveyor of the Queen's Pictures Sir Oliver Millar records, 'The collection formed by the rulers of Britain, from the Tudors to the present time . . . reflects their discernment and prejudice, their bad taste as well as their good, their friendships, diversions, loves, hates, idiosyncrasies and obsessions in a uniquely illuminating manner.'

It would be easy for members of the royal family to be suffocated by their matchless heritage so that they would be indifferent to

---

*An idea of the astronomical value of the Royal Collection may be gained by comparing the sale for £20 million ($34 million) of the Duke of Devonshire's collection of 70 Old Master drawings and sketches. Art experts regarded this private collection as second only to the Royal Collection in size and value. The Queen has 600 drawings by Leonardo da Vinci alone including his miraculous Head of St Anne. If, in the words of former Prime Minister, the late Lord Stockton, the present Government decided to sell 'the family silver' of some 35,000 important drawings and paintings they would raise around £9 billion ($15.3 billion) – the amount they received from the sales of shares in both British Telecom and British Gas. As a caveat if the entire Royal Collection came on to the market at the same time, it would considerably reduce its value.

their own opportunity to make a contribution. Yet the collections of furniture, silverware, gold plate and porcelain are just as comprehensive and breathtaking as the Royal Collection of paintings.

For example, the justly famous Sèvres service made for King Louis XVI of France and bought by George IV for £40,000 ($200,000) is the crowning glory of the Royal Collection of porcelain. And, on a different note Prince Charles has made a whimsical assembly of Victorian and Edwardian lavatories, while the Princess of Wales has a growing collection of charming Crummles boxes and Wemyes ware animals – a sign that royal collecting is still flourishing.

Perhaps the one collection which has no associations with previous reigns is the car museum at Sandringham. The royal family took to the automobile early on. As Prince of Wales, Edward VII enjoyed his first ride in February 1896 in the grounds of the Imperial Institute in Kensington. Two years later a trip in a Daimler with Lord Montagu of Beaulieu convinced him that it was time that every self-respecting monarch ought to possess a motor vehicle.

Shortly after his Coronation he began to buy his own cars, including a Mercedes and a

George V and Queen Mary in a royal limousine. Note the royal crest painted on the door.

Renault, painted in distinctive claret with fine red lilies picked out on the bodywork. Queen Alexandra had exacting requests for her own Daimlers which were mainly used for taking her six children on picnics. Her specifications included silk blinds, a watch case and ornate mother of pearl fittings.

After one day out in Sandringham the exhilarated Queen wrote to her eldest son, 'I did enjoy being driven about in the cool of the evening at 50 miles!! an hour! – when nothing in the way of course only! – and I must say I have the greatest confidence in our driver – I poke him violently in the back at every corner to go gently when ever a dog, child or anything comes in our way.'

King Edward VII took his limousines abroad but despite his love of motoring he remained lamentably ignorant about the workings of the internal combustion engine. He once found himself unable to tell the Kaiser what fuel cars used. The German ruler was equally vague, suggesting potato spirit rather than petrol.

While the royal family have treated their cars much like their horses – the working cars are 'stabled' in the Royal Mews under the Crown Equerry who is also responsible for the thirty horses – they have displayed exacting and extravagant tastes towards their carriages.

George V insisted that he should enter his Daimler without bending his head and had a

The Duke of York is driven through London in an open-topped Bianchi car.

six-wheel vehicle built that could travel over the ploughed fields at Sandringham and let him shoot birds while remaining seated. Queen Mary demanded a Daimler that incorporated an air-conditioning system that would rid the interior of the King's cigarette smoke without blowing cold air onto his head.

After the war, George VI threw economy to the wind and ordered two new matching Daimlers, complete with electric glove warmers and a special hat peg for the Queen, to add to his collection of fourteen royal cars.

The present Queen's first car was a Daimler presented to her by her parents on her eighteenth birthday. She was so devoted to the car that she even had it shipped to Malta in 1949 where she joined the Duke of Edinburgh on his naval duties. The registration number – JGY 280 – has been transferred to her other private cars ever since. Unlike George V who thought driving motor vehicles was undignified, the Queen has even been spotted driving the green staff bus with its chattering collection of

cleaners from Balmoral to the nearby village of Ballater.

The Queen has received a number of cars as gifts of which the most handsome was a Rolls-Royce Phantom VI, presented to her by the British motor industry to celebrate her Silver Jubilee in 1977. It was specially designed so that it could fit on board the royal yacht *Britannia.* Unlike the interiors of other Phantoms, this £250,000 ($425,000) limousine has no television set or cocktail cabinet. Instead there is a veneered cassette holder for the Queen's favourite tapes – music by the band of the Brigade of Guards. Above this is an Asprey clock, and in the extra wide central arm rest, a pocket dictation machine, radio cassette player and a large mirror on a swivel. The rear seat rises an extra three and a half inches so that the public can get a better view of the Queen on public engagements.

Until recently most royal cars were sold in part exchange for new ones. Very few were consciously retained as articles of historic or technical importance – even as late as 1942 George VI donated Edward VII's first car to the Daimler museum in Coventry. As a result

ABOVE: *The unique royal Rolls Royce Phantom VI was a Silver Jubilee gift to the Queen in 1977.* LEFT: *The ceremonial St George and the Dragon mascot.*

scores of wonderful old vehicles were stripped of their royal identity, the august claret and gold exterior was painted over, armorial bearings removed, index numbers re-registered and even log books deposited with local authorities with instructions to refuse information to all inquirers. In this manner they were sold off anonymously and lost sight of. A Leeds housewife for instance was seen driving one of the Princess of Wales' Ford Escort runabouts.

It was not until some twenty years ago that the present Queen decided that royal motorized transport had a heritage value of its own and in 1968 persuaded Daimler to part with four vehicles once owned by the royal family — including the 1900 Daimler which her father had given them twenty-six years before. They formed the nucleus of the current collection at the Royal Motor Museum at Sandringham which now consists of seventeen vehicles, all restored to their former glory. By 1975 the Queen had given orders that none of the principal State cars — mostly Rolls-Royces — should be disposed of again. Instead they are

ABOVE: *Interior of the Phantom VI. Music by the band of the Brigade of Guards is always to hand.*
RIGHT: *The Queen's standard and coat of arms.*

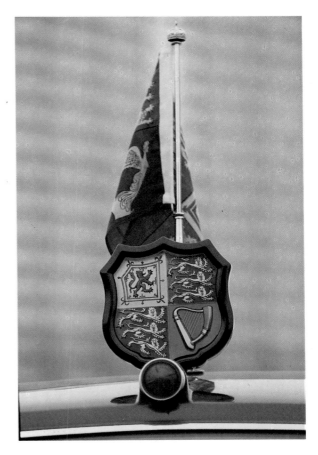

now sent to Sandringham when they have outlived their usefulness.

This fledgling private collection is reckoned by Peter Card, the vintage car valuer at ADT auctions to be worth £250,000 ($425,000), not much when set against the royal family's overall wealth. Royal associations clearly affect the re-sale value of cars – for example a twenty-seven-year-old Rolls Royce Phantom V, once owned by the Queen Mother but since bought by a Lancashire businessman, was recently auctioned for £100,000 ($170,000) because of its royal pedigree.

The Sovereign's car is distinguished from other road users by the absence of number plates and road tax. Speed restrictions do not apply although, against much grumbling from Edward VII, royal vehicles must be insured against accident. Other members of the royal family must obey every traffic law as both the Princess Royal and Captain Mark Phillips have found to their cost.

In 1913 George V decreed that the Sovereign's official car should have the Royal

Standard pennanted to it and that his chauffeur should wear distinctive scarlet livery. He had already adopted his own symbol of recognition by accepting a silver figure of Britannia with the lion at its feet for the bonnet. George VI chose a lion mascot which the Queen Mother continues to use to this day. The Queen's official Rolls-Royce has a silver ceremonial model of St George and the Dragon. It has a sentimental history – the figure first stood on top of her wedding cake.

Indeed the secret of the success of the House of Windsor has been the ability to invest the mundane with the mystery and magnificence that is monarchy.

The real driving force behind their phenomenal success over the last 150 years has been the wealth of tribute which has flowed into their coffers. They are a family without any visible means of support, an endless high wire act sustained, not by a safety net anchored in commerce, but by the will of the watching millions.

Their dynasty survives because we wish it to continue. The tribute they accept has outgrown European royalty as well as the British Empire and is now on an international scale. The Windsors are the first truly international family. Long after President Bush and Mrs Thatcher have left the world stage, the House of Windsor will continue to fascinate and absorb.

The achievement of the Windsor dynasty has been to overlay a patina of duty, responsibility and guardianship over the cracked and faded edifice of monarchy, turning it from a bankrupt, largely discredited Estate into the thriving, near impregnable institution it is today. Their self image of financial deprivation has reinforced their ascendancy. As long as Prince Charles chaffs at the price of hay for his polo ponies and the Queen does not obviously flaunt her great dynastic fortune, then her subjects are happy to give them their trust, their deference and their loyalty.

At the same time the present royal House lives in a world where, as George V once remarked, 'Everything here is of the best.' Their personal collections of jewellery, Fabergé, furniture and *objets d'art* are the finest in the world, a kingdom built on the flow of tribute which endlessly celebrates their universal celebrity and status.

Truly their glory has made their kingdom.

Appendix

A. JEWELLERY

The private royal jewellery was valued for this book by Mr Laurence Krashes, for sixteen years the senior assessor for Harry Winston and author of *Harry Winston: The Ultimate Jeweler*. As the Queen has not yet allowed any gemological study to be made of her private collection the task was, in his words, 'like landing a plane in fog without radar.'

His assessment is based on the cut, setting and quality of the stones. The royal pedigree would automatically add a factor of ten to the price of any piece which came on the commercial market. While this has been taken into account when making the final estimate of the royal family's wealth, this was not a component in Mr Krashes' valuation. (£1 = $1.70)

Diamonds

Queen Mary 'Girls of Great Britain and Ireland' tiara	£382,000 (650,000)
Sun Ray tiara	£294,000 ($500,000)
Queen Alexandra Russian tiara	£530,000 ($900,000)
Delhi Durbar tiara (last seen 1911)	£353,000 ($600,000)
Scroll tiara	£235,000 ($400,000)
Queen Mary floret earrings	£177,000 ($300,000)
Queen Mary cluster earrings	£177,000 ($300,000)
Queen Victoria stud earrings	£118,000 ($200,00)
Queen Elizabeth II pearshape earrings	£294,000 ($500,000)
King George VI chandelier earrings	£235,000 ($400,000)
Festoon diamond necklace	£735,000 ($1,250,000)
Queen Victoria collet necklace and earrings	£1,176,00 ($2,000,000)
'My best diamonds' necklace	£662,000 ($1,125,000)
King Faisal of Saudi Arabia necklace	£447,000 ($760,000)
King Khalid necklace	£412,000 ($700,00)
Williamson diamond pin	£2,353,000 ($4,000,000)
Queen Victoria bow brooches	£44,000 ($75,000)
Jardinière and basket brooch	£44,000 ($75,000)
Ivy leaf brooch	£59,000 ($10,00)
Maple leaf brooch	£24,000 ($40,000)
Queen Mary Dorset bow brooch	£24,000 ($40,000)
Queen Victoria bar brooch	£88,000 ($150,000)
Queen Mary stomacher	£882,000 ($1,500,000)
Queen Mary true lover's knot brooch	£44,000 ($75,000)
King William IV brooch	£74,000 ($125,000)
Queen Victoria wheat ear brooch	£26,500 ($45,000)
Resille Collar (last seen in 1930s)	£588,300 ($1,000,000)
Various diamond family orders	£588,300 ($1,000,000)
Switzerland Federal Republic watch	£44,000 ($75,000)
King William IV buckle bracelets	£118,000 ($200,000)
Queen Mary link bracelets	£132,000 ($225,000)
Queen Mary Indian bangle bracelets	£120,000 ($205,000)
Queen Elizabeth II's modern bracelet	£103,000 ($175,000)
Queen Elizabeth II engagement ring	£74,000 ($125,000)
Prince Philip wedding bracelet	£153,000 ($260,000)
Assorted gift pins	£265,000 ($450,000)
Cullinan III, 94.40 carat, pearshape	£5,588,000 ($9,500,000)
Cullinan IV, 63.60 carat, emerald cut	£3,741,000 ($6,360,000)
Cullinan V heart-shape brooch	£530,000 ($900,000)
Cullinan VI marquise diamond	£271,000 ($460,000)
Cullinan VII and VIII brooch	£441,000 ($750,000)
Cullinan necklace	£265,000 ($450,000)
TOTAL	**£22,875,294 ($38,885,000)**

Emeralds

Cambridge and Delhi Durbar parure	£1,470,000 ($2,500,000)
Cambridge emeralds and Grand Duchess Vladimir pearl and diamond tiara	£1,470,000 ($2,500,000)
Cambridge emerald brooches	£412,000 ($700,000)
Queen Mary art deco bracelet	£103,000 ($175,000)
Queen Victoria fringe earrings and Godman necklace	£324,000 ($550,000)
Carved Indian emerald brooch	£206,000 ($350,000)
Indian emerald girdle	£1,765,000 ($3,000,000)
TOTAL	**£5,750,000 ($9,775,000)**

Pearls

Queen Anne and Queen Caroline necklace	£588,300 ($1,000,000)
Queen Elizabeth II four row choker	£29,400 ($50,000)
Empress Marie Feodorovna of Russia necklace	£118,000 ($200,000)
Queen Alexandra's bracelet	£118,000 ($200,000)
Queen Mary pearl and diamond bracelet	£206,000 ($350,000)
Cambridge lover's knot tiara	£471,000 ($800,000)
Queen Victoria Golden Jubilee necklace	£177,000 ($300,000)
Queen Mary pendant earrings	£88,000 ($150,000)

Duchess of Teck earrings	£29,400 ($50,000)	
Queen Victoria drop earrings	£59,000 ($100,000)	
Queen Alexandra cluster earrings	£44,000 ($75,000)	
Queen Mary button earrings	£18,000 ($30,000)	
Queen Alexandra Dagmar necklace	£206,000 ($350,000)	
Queen Alexandra triple drop brooch and necklace	£265,000 ($450,000)	
Queen Mary 'Woman of Hampshire' pendant brooch	£103,000 ($175,000)	
Queen Mary bar brooch	£44,000 ($75,000)	
Duchess of Teck corsage brooch	£88,000 ($150,000)	
Duchess of Cambridge pendant brooch	£118,000 ($200,000)	
Queen Mary Kensington bow brooch and Warwick bow brooch	£147,000 ($250,000)	
Amir of Qatar necklace	£177,000 ($300,000)	
Queen Elizabeth, the Queen Mother, flower brooch	£44,000 ($75,000)	
Princess Marie Louise bracelet	£132,000 ($225,000)	
TOTAL	**£3,265,000 ($5,555,000)**	

Sapphires

King George VI Victoria suite	£471,000 ($800,000)
Sapphire tiara	£280,000 ($475,000)
Prince Albert brooch	£103,000 ($175,000)
Empress Marie Feodorovna of Russia brooch	£294,000 ($500,000)
Queen Elizabeth, the Queen Mother, leaf brooch	£24,000 ($40,000)
Queen Elizabeth II flower spray brooch	£8,800 ($15,000)
Queen Elizabeth II set of flower clips	£20,500 ($35,000)
Queen Mary Russian brooch	£118,000 ($200,000)
Queen Elizabeth II 18th birthday present	£103,000 ($175,000)
TOTAL	**£1,420,000 ($2,415,000)**

Rubies

Queen Mary, Rose of York bracelet	£530,000 ($900,000)
Queen Mary cluster earrings	£206,000 ($350,000)
King George VI bandeau necklace	£412,000 ($700,000)
Art deco bracelet	£132,000 ($225,000)
Queen Elizabeth, the Queen Mother bracelet	£71,000 ($120,000)
TOTAL	**£1,350,000 ($2,295,000)**

A minimum of £1,000,000 ($1,700,000) must be allowed to cover the less precious jewels such as the aquamarine set given to the Queen by the Brazilian Government, the Duchess of Kent amethyst suite, the Queen's aquamarine and diamond clip as well as other topaz pieces.

GRAND TOTAL   £35,661,294 ($60,625,000)

B. LAND

Crown Estate

These lands are part of the Sovereign's hereditary possessions – 'right of Crown' – and are neither property of the Government nor the Queen. They exist in an untested, though profitable, legal no man's land administered by a twelve-man Crown Estate Commission.

In June 1988 the Report of the Comptroller of the Auditor General of the Crown Estates valued the estate's assets at £1.2 billion. This figure has not been incorporated into the overall wealth of the royal family although, as we have seen, the Crown Estate occupies a confusing position regarding ownership.

Properties range from Trafalgar Square and shops in Regent Street in London, forests in Scotland, the Windsor Great Park and mineral rights on the coastal seabed.

The Crown Estate's value is made up of the following: (Figures in millions)

1. London properties

Regent Street	£190 ($323)
Lower Regent Street	£88 ($150)
City	£107 ($182)
Kensington	£87 ($148)
St James's	£82 ($140)
Regent's Park	£80 ($136)
Millbank	£73 ($124)
Victoria Street	£66 ($112)
South Pall Mall	£55 ($94)
Wardour Street	£43 ($73)
TOTAL	**£871 ($1480)**

2. Provinces

The 'old provincial portfolio' is concentrated around Windsor and Ascot with a small number of holdings elsewhere in the south of England.

Value: £45 ($77)

3. The 'diversification portfolio'

This includes a business park in Cambridge and a shopping centre at High Wycombe.

Value: £55 ($93)

4. The 'agricultural estate'

This consists of 270,000 acres in England and Wales and 600 tenancies.

Value: £137.5 ($234)

5. The forestry estate

This comprises ten separate sites.

Value: £11 ($19)

6. The foreshore, seabed and mineral estate

This includes 55 per cent of the coastal foreshore, all the seabed within territorial waters and the right to explore the continental shelf outside territorial waters. Ownership excludes oil and gas rights, which belong to the Department of Energy, and coal rights which belong to British Coal.

Value: £37.4 ($64)

7. Duchy of Lancaster

The Queen retains the tax-free income from the Duchy which, in 1988, amounted to £2,270,000 ($3,859,000). In 1988 a confidential 40-page report was being prepared on the Duchy which will recommend wide ranging changes in the administration of these ancient lands.

Indications of the future modernization programme came in the Duchy of Lancaster Act 1988 which extended the leasing powers of the Chancellor (normally a high-ranking government minister) and Council of the Duchy of Lancaster. Under the terms of the act, the Chancellor and Council may lease land but no lease shall be granted unless the best 'consideration in money or money's worth can be obtained' or the lease is for public or charitable purposes.

The bulk of the 50,000-acre estate, mainly in Yorkshire, Lancashire, Cheshire and Staffordshire, is agricultural. However, there are small property interests in London, Northamptonshire and Ogmore, Mid-Glamorgan.

While the Duchy files annual accounts to Parliament, no accurate valuation has been recently attempted. For this book the annual reports of the Duchies of Lancaster and Cornwall were examined as well as the Inland Revenue's Property Market Report which values land by geography and type and so proved a valuable indicator of the worth of private royal estates. At the same time surveyors, estate agents and, in Scotland, local factors, were consulted for their expert local knowledge of land prices. The cachet of owning royal estates was omitted from the commercial equation.

The 50,000 acres of the Duchy of Lancaster has a lower value than expected because of the high number of long or 'roll over' leases.

Value: £55 million ($94 million)

8. Balmoral

A 50,00-acre estate in Grampian, Scotland. It comprises lands surrounding Balmoral Castle and nearby Birkhall, Queen Elizabeth, the Queen Mother's lodge, together with 7,600 acres at Delnadamph purchased in 1977 and 5,000 acres held at Bachnagairn in neighbouring Tayside.

During the present reign the Castle and estate have been modernized and improved, reflecting a corresponding increase in value. While much of the estate is poor quality upland – worth £200 to £300 ($340-$510) an acre – the land also boasts excellent hunting, shooting and fishing. The royal estate has over one hundred head of red deer with a capital value of £15,000 ($25,000) each while the grouse alone are worth between £7 and £10 million ($11.9 and 417 million). Fishing rights on the River Dee which bounds the estate are estimated on the basis of £5,000 ($8,500) each salmon. The castle, lodges, stables and immediate grounds are worth around £5 million ($8.5 million).

Estate value: £35-£40 million ($60-$68 million)

9. Sandringham

The 20,000-acre estate is now an efficiently managed unit comprising the 270-roomed mansion itself as well as Anmer Hall (until recently the country home of the Duke and Duchess of Kent) numerous tenanted cottages, tenanted farms, a thoroughbred stud, gun dog kennels and extensive shooting rights. Estate valuation: £55–60 million ($93.5–102 million) with the House and gardens valued at £15 million ($25.5 million).

10. Racing stables, West Ilsley, Berkshire

Purchased in 1982 for around £800,000 ($1.85 million) the stables comprise the main house, cottages and stables set in 100 acres of land.

Estate valuation: £1.5 million ($2.55 million)

11. Duchy of Cornwall

Since 1337 the Duchy of Cornwall has provided the main source of income and investment for all Princes of Wales. The estate comprises 120,000 acres spread over 20 counties. As with the Duchy of Lancaster, the annual published accounts give no accurate valuation as the land is a complicated and ancient mix of parcels of hill top estate as well as tenanted property.

It comprises the following holdings:

Devon	72,489 acres
Cornwall	21,546 acres
Isles of Scilly	3,984 acres
Avon	8,919 acres
Somerset	7,112 acres
Wiltshire	4,575 acres
Dorset	2,798 acres
Lincolnshire	1,936 acres
Gloucestershire	1,864 acres
London	41 acres mainly in Kennington, south London, including the Oval cricket ground.

The London property is by far the most valuable. An indication was given in 1987 when the sale of Newquay House, Kennington raised £1.2 million ($2.04 million) and two other London properties a further £1.9 million ($3.23 million).

Duchy value: £250 million (425 million)

In the year ended 1987 the Prince's annual income from the Duchy was £1.9 million ($3.23 million) while his stock market portfolio amounted to £19.7 million ($33.49 million).

His nine-bedroomed country home, Highgrove set in 347 acres of Gloucestershire farmland was purchased for £800,000 ($1.85 million) in 1980. The Prince has added 400 acres to the existing farmland. At today's prices the property is valued at £3.2 million ($5.44 million).

C. MOTOR VEHICLES

There are currently seventeen motor vehicles exhibited at the privately owned Sandringham Motor Museum on the Queen's Norfolk estate. They were independently assessed for this book by Mr Peter Card, the senior vintage car valuer at A.D.T Auctions, Bedford. The value of the cars does not take into account the cachet of royal ownership. In total the seventeen vehicles are worth £250,000 ($425,000) while the registration plates are valued at £52,000 ($88,400).

The value of each vehicle is as follows:

1900 Daimler (Tonneau)	£40,000 ($68,000)
1913 Daimler (Brougham)	£35,000 ($59 5000)
1954 Rolls-Royce Phantom IV	£30,000 ($51,000)
1924 Daimler (Shooting Brake)	£25,000 ($42,500)
1929 Daimler (Brougham)	£25,000 ($42,500)
1936 Daimler (Shooting Brake)	£20,000 ($34,000)
1961 Alvis T.D. 21	£10,000 ($17,000)
1939 Merryweather Fire Engine	£8,000 ($13,600)
1949 Daimler (Limousine)	£6,000 ($10,200)
1947 Daimler (Saloon)	£5,000 ($8,500)
1949 Ford Pilot Shooting Brake	£4,000 ($6,800)
1968 M.G.C. (G.T.)	£4,000 ($6,800)
1969 Austin Princess Vanden Plas	£3,000 ($5,100)
1961 Vauxhall Cresta estate	£3,000 ($5,100)
1963 Rover 3 litre saloon	£3,000 ($5,100)
1966 Land Rover station wagon	£3,000 ($5,100)
1956 Ford Zephyr	£3,000 ($5,100)

D. HORSE RACING

The sport of kings is very much a lottery, the value of a stable changing dramatically depending on the fortunes of the horses in training. For example in 1982 the Queen sold her outstanding filly, Height of Fashion, to Sheik Maktoum for an estimated £1.25 million. Since then this classic mare has produced three high class group winners, Al Wasmi, Unfuwain and Nashwan, which won the 2,000 Guineas in 1989.

The racing success of these three horses gives them a prize tag of well over £25 million – a shrewd investment for Sheik Maktoum. As one racing expert commented: 'The Queen must be kicking herself for selling Height of Fashion.'

In the 1989 season the Queen had thirty-one horses in training worth around £750,000 ($1,275,000), twenty-three brood mares and their foals, worth about £1,750,000 ($2,975,000) and fifteen yearlings with a market value of £225,000 ($382,500). As well as her immediate stable the Queen also holds nineteen stallion shares – Shirley Heights and Bustino form the majority – which adds a further £500,000 ($850,000).

A London company of bloodstock dealers estimate that the Queen has made an investment of between £3,000,000 ($4.5 million) and £3,500,000 ($5.95 million) in pedigree horseflesh. If she had kept Height of Fashion the value of her stable would be at least ten times that figure.

The annual running costs of her stables will, according to reputable thoroughbred agents, be upwards of £600,000 ($1,020,000). A horse in training costs £12,000 ($20,400) a year to maintain while brood mares and yearlings between £5,000 ($8,500) and £6,000 ($10,200) each. This expenditure is offset at West Ilsley stables by training and stabling horses for competing owners.

Illustration Sources

Alpha: (Photo Julian Herbert), 133 (Photo Judy Appelbee), 162 (Photo Jim Bennett); The Bridgeman Art Library, London: 35, 36–7 (Forbes Magazine Collection, New York), 38, 39 (Guildhall Library Collection, London), 55 (Bonhams, London), 62–3 (Roy Miles Gallery, London), 67 (House of Lords), 69 (The Royal & Ancient Golf Club, St Andrews), 98 (The Institute of Directors, London); Camera Press, London: 15, 77, 103 (right) (Photos Baron), 22 (Photo Norman Parkinson), 25 (Photo S. Djukanovic), 28, 125 (Photos Cecil Beaton), 31 (Illustrated London News), 79 (Photo Marcus Adams), 109, 129, 131, 148–9 (Photos Patrick Lichfield), 116, (Photo Snowdon), 124 (Photo Anthony Crickmay), 136 (Photo Glenn Harvey), 155 (Photo HRH Prince Andrew); Lionel Cherruault: 88; Reproduced by Permission of the Controller of Her Majesty's Stationery Office: 83, 106, 107, 108; Reginald Davis: 118, 134–5; Tim Graham, London: 7, 12, 13, 16, 17, 24, 30, 31, 33, 80, 81, 89, 90, 91, 95, 101 (2), 102, 104, 113, 119, 120 (2), 121, 126, 132, 138–9, 140, 154 (above), 163, 166 (2), 167 (2), 169; Robert Harding Associates, London: 49, 51; Reproduced by Gracious permission of Her Majesty the Queen: 6, 8–9, 32, 41, 46–7, 61, 157, 158 (2), 159; The Hulton-Deutsch Collection: 154 (below); Anwar Hussein: 128, 130; Illustrated London News Picture Library: 20, 60, 68, 94, 100, 112 (right), 160; JS Library: 48, 96 (below); 147; The Law & Dunbar-Nasmith Partnership, Edinburgh: 26–7; The Mansell Collection, London: 40, 44, 58, 143; Mary Evans Picture Library, London: 22, 42, 53, 142, 165; Robin Nunn: 110, 123, 127; Photographers International: 97, 103 (left) (Photo by Jayne Fincher); Pilgrim Press Ltd, Derby: 161; Popperfoto: 10, 11, 14, 18, 19, 45, 54, 57, 59, 65, 72, 74, 85, 92, 111, 145, 152, 153, 164; Rex Features Ltd: 99; Sandringham, Lord Chamberlain's Office: 137, 141; Courtesy of Sotheby's: 70, 71, 75, 76; Syndication International Ltd, London: 50, 82, 96 (above), 146; 151; Topham Picture library: 73; Victoria & Albert Museum, London: 114, 115 (Cecil Beaton Estate); Wartski Jewellers Ltd, London: 93 (Photo John Lilley), 112 (left)

Bibliography

Arthur, Sir George: *Concerning Queen Victoria and Her Son* (The Right Book Club, 1945)

Ashton, Sir Leigh: *Guide to Queen Mary's Art Treasures* (Victoria and Albert Museum)

Barry, Stephen: *Royal Secrets* (Villard, 1985)

Battiscombe, Georgina: *Queen Alexandra* (Constable, 1969)

Bloch, Michael: *The Secret File of the Duke of Windsor* (Bantam Press, 1988)

Boothroyd, Basil: *Philip* (Longman, 1971)

Channon, Sir Henry: *Chips: The Diaries of Sir Henry Channon* (Weidenfeld and Nicolson, 1967)

Colville, Lady Cynthia: *Crowded Life* (Evans Brothers, 1963)

Connell, B.: *Manifest Destiny* (Cassell, 1953)

Crossman, Richard: *The Diaries of a Cabinet Minister*, Vol II (Hamish Hamilton and Jonathan Cape, 1976)

Donaldson, Frances: *Edward VIII* (Weidenfeld and Nicolson, 1986)

Duff, David: *The Shy Princess* (Muller, 1974)

Duff, David: *Alexandra, Princess and Queen* (Collins, 1980)

Edwards, Anne: *Matriarch* (Hodder and Stoughton, 1984)

Edwards, Ann: *The Queen's Clothes* (Beaverbrook Newspapers 1977)

Field, Leslie: *The Queen's Jewels* (Weidenfeld and Nicolson, 1987)

Fox, Mike and Smith, Steve: *Rolls Royce, the Complete Works* (Faber and Faber, 1984)

Garrett, Richard: *Royal Travel* (Blandford Press, 1982)

Hammer, Armand: *Witness to History* (Coronet, 1988)

Menkes, Suzy: *The Royal Jewels* (Grafton Books, 1985)

Morrow, Ann: *Highness, the Maharajahs of India* (Grafton, 1986)

Morton, Andrew: *The Royal Yacht* Britannia (Orbis, 1984)

Morton, Andrew: *Inside Kensington Palace* (Michael O'Mara, 1987)

Morton, Andrew: *Duchess* (Michael O'Mara, 1988)

Nash, Michael: *The Strange Case of the Royal Wills*, (Unpublished), Cambridge, 1984)

Pearson, John: *The Ultimate Family* (Michael Joseph, 1986)

Plum, J.H. and Huw Wheldon: *Royal Heritage* (BBC, 1977)

Ponsonby, Sir Frederick: *Recollection of Three Reigns* (Eyre and Spottiswoode, 1951)

Pope-Hennessy, James: *Queen Mary 1867–1953* (George Allen and Unwin, 1959)

Randall, David: *Royal Follies* (W.H. Allen, 1987)

Rose, Kenneth: *George V* (Weidenfeld and Nicolson, 1983)

Select Committee on the Civil List, 1971–1972 (HMSO, 1971)

Servants, One of Her Majesty's (Anon): *The Private Life of the Queen* (Gresham Books, 1897)

Seth-Smith, Michael: *Bred for the Purple* (Leslie Frewin, 1969)

Smith, Brian: *Royal Daimlers* (Transport Bookman, 1979)

Snowman, Kenneth: *Fabergé 1846–1920* (Debrett/Victoria and Albert Museum

Thornton, Michael: *Royal Feud* (Michael Joseph, 1985)

Victoria, Queen: *The Letters of Queen Victoria*, Second Series, Vols I, II, *1862–1878*, (Murray, 1925)

Whitlock, Ralph: *Royal Farmers* (Michael Joseph, 1980)

Wilson, Sir John: *The Royal Philatelic Collection* (Dropmore Press, 1952)

Windsor, H.R.H. the Duke of: *A King's Story* (Cassell, 1951)

Author's Acknowledgements

I am grateful to the Trustees of the Broadlands Archive Trust for permission to quote from Sir Ernest Cassel's papers held at Southampton University and to Queen's University Archives, Kingston, Canada for giving me access to Sir Edward Peacock's papers.

The valuation of jewellery and *objets d'art* by Laurence Krashes, a senior assessor for Harry Winston in New York, has been invaluable as too has been the work of investment analyst Sharon Kelly who managed to penetrate the secrecy of the Bank of England Nominees where most of the royal stocks and shares are held. Property journalist Anne Caborn used her extensive contacts to give a realistic valuation of the royal estates, Michael Nash, senior law lecturer at Norwich City College defined the private and public royal property, Peter Card, vintage car dealer at A.D.T. Auctions, Bedford assessed the royal motor vehicles while Trevor Hall's digging into the hidden corners of royal history uncovered a number of gems.

I have had considerable help and advice from those who work or have worked behind the Palace walls. Inevitably they must remain anonymous but my gratitude is no less heartfelt. My thanks also to Sharada Dwivedi in Bombay and Lubna Hussain in London for their work on the Indian royal families as well as Alan Hamilton, Suzy Menkes, James Rusbridger, Patricia Smith, Dr Christopher Woolgar, archivist, Southampton University, Paul Bamfield, assistant archivist, Queen's University, and the librarians at the Press Association, *New Statesmen*, *Morning Star*, *Illustrated London News*, and the *Burlington* and *Majesty* magazines. The enthusiasm of Michael O'Mara, who hosted the classic publisher's lunch which launched this project, has been, as ever inspirational while the support of my wife, Lynne has been beyond the price of rubies.

Andrew Morton
March, 1989

Index